Bets and the City

Sally Nicoll's spread betting diary

D1387016

Harriman House Ltd
3A Penns Road
Petersfield
Hampshire
GU32 2EW

Tel. +44 (0)1730 233870
Fax +44(0)1730 233880
Email: enquiries@harriman-house.com
Website: www.harriman-house.com

First published in Great Britain in 2006 by Harriman House Ltd.
Reprinted 2007 and 2008
Copyright © Harriman House Ltd

ISBN 1-905-64106-0
ISBN13 978-1905641-06-2

British Library Cataloguing in Publication Data
A CIP catalogue record for this book can be obtained from the British Library

Printed and bound by the CPI Group, Antony Rowe.

The storyline and opinions expressed in Bets and the City are solely and
independently those of the author and are not influenced by the employees or
agents of Finspreads. You should not assume that the contents of my book
necessarily reflect the views of Finspreads.

Finspreads, which is a trading name of IFX Markets Ltd, engaged me to keep
and publish my diary on their website. Although, they exercised no editorial
control over the contents other than to assist me in meeting FSA regulatory
requirements. As a precautionary measure, I have been made an appointed
representative of IFX Markets Ltd in relation to the publication of this book and
the £50 promotion.

Bets and the City is for Gareth.

And for my dad, who would have loved it.

A message from Sally:
Spread betting is high risk. You can lose your shirt and more besides. So please be careful, and don't get carried away.

In the diary

The Diary

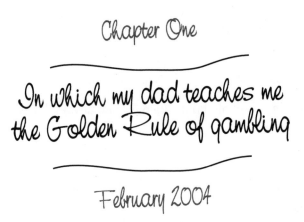

Chapter One

In which my dad teaches me the Golden Rule of gambling

February 2004

It all began one Sunday in Portsmouth, around the time Duran Duran were making regular appearances on *Top of the Pops*.

"Now then," said my dad. "If you score more than 1000 points on this pinball machine, I'll give you 50p and another glass of Tizer. But if you get less than 500, you lose 10p from this week's pocket money."

This, I suppose, was my very first spread bet: I rose immediately to the challenge. Fifty pence was well worth having, and the fear of losing didn't even enter my head.

It was ten years before I would legitimately be able to order a vodka and Red Bull, but already I was the *Star & Garter's* resident Sunday lunchtime pinball wizard. I had my own little beer crate that I used to stand on to get a better view of the table and the angles. And God, I was good. People used to stand, watch and cheer me on.

Even so, 1000 points on a machine where you needed 800 just to get a replay was a tall order.

My first game: 650 points. The second: 950.

"Time we were off home then." Dad always knew how to motivate me.

Game three: 1,275 points.

It wasn't until the following Tuesday that my father confessed the pub had a High Score Promotion in play, and my prowess had won him £5 and a packet of Players cigarettes.

We became partners in crime. The weekly (most weeks) 50p became my first regular income.

After a couple of months had passed, I renegotiated my share of the box office. At which point dad reckoned I was ready for the next stage of what he called my Alternative Education.

This consisted of two subjects.

Firstly, football. Which necessitated spending every other Saturday on the terraces at Fratton Park. Here, I learned virtues such as patience, optimism, instant wit and repartee, public speaking – "Why's the referee always on THEIR side?" – a love of trivia (bet you didn't know Sir Arthur Conan Doyle was Pompey's first-ever goalkeeper), plus resilience in the face of habitual failure.

Our father-daughter tribulations were punctuated by regular visits to Plumpton, Goodwood, Brighton, Lingfield and my favourite race course of them all, Fontwell Park, where a horse called Highland Bounty romped home at outrageous odds, ensuring I was hooked forever.

By the time I had my nose stuck into *The Sporting Life* – while my classmates studied *Jane Eyre*, *Romeo and Juliet*, and *Cosmopolitan* – I was ready for my next BIG lesson.

"I want to bet on that one over there." I pointed to my choice in the parade ring at Fontwell, prior to the last race of the day.

"Bad idea. It's sweating up," dad advised.

But I insisted, emptied my pockets, and exchanged all my money for a bookie's betting slip.

Ten minutes later, the horse trailed in last. Normally, my dad would compensate me on a losing bet – he was a softie that way – but this time, no refund was forthcoming.

I sulked all the way back to Chichester. This was No Fun. Finally, dad broke the silence, and delivered one of the most important pieces of advice I have ever been fortunate enough to receive:

"When you go to the races, never take out of the house more money than you can afford to throw into the gutter."

Which all these years later has morphed into some of my dearest friends looking at me with horror and saying

"Spread WHAT? You've got to be kidding!"

Chapter Two

To make £1 million, all I need is a computer and an Internet connection

March 2004

This is what happened.

I have been unemployable for several years. Not because I am talentless, but because I'm not much of a team player. That's what they told me when they showed me the door of the advertising agency where I'd been working since leaving Uni.

My crime? I had merely presented a client with a copy of the Bible, in order to prove my point that it is perfectly permissible to start sentences with words like 'and' and 'but'.

"The trouble with you, Sally," said the creative director, "is that not only do you not suffer fools gladly, you also don't suffer quite intelligent people gladly." I resisted the temptation to tell him there were far too many negatives in the sentence, gleefully grabbed my enormous severance pay – were they really that keen to see the last of me? – and immediately set up on my own.

The girl done good.

While dad nurtured my love of gambling and encouraged me to take calculated risks, my mum's puritan work ethic also rubbed off. Weeks of frenzied activity would be followed by days of frenzied inactivity. I was a success. Three holidays a year, a season ticket for Spurs (Portsmouth was my first love, but Tottenham's the team I married), even the cliché of a little red sports car.

So on New Year's Eve, when I announced I was jacking it all in to become a novelist, some of my dearest friends looked at me with horror and chorused, "Write a BOOK? You've got to be kidding!"

So far, I have written 20,000 words. The car's been swapped for a bicycle, and my life savings – I've always been a saver rather than a spender – will allow me to live a trimmed yet essentially comfortable life for the next couple of years. This is fortunate, because although I am prepared to make certain sacrifices – shopping at Morrisons, rather than Waitrose and Fresh and Wild – I have no wish to starve in a garret.

The good thing about being a novelist is that you get to drink a lot of coffee during normal working hours. There are a lot of self-employed – and self-unemployed – people in my part of London, and we gravitate instinctively towards one another in the local cafes.

Last Wednesday, I'm sitting with assorted members of the Primrose Hill latterati. Don the Drug Dealer, is boasting how much he's making by spread betting cricket scores. My curiosity is piqued; I am sure I can do the same with soccer – most Saturdays I can double my money on the fixed odds coupon (stick to picking three home wins and don't let the bookies beguile you with their promise of 15/1 for seven results) and this will make a nice change.

That afternoon, instead of completing chapter six, I Google "spread betting".

There's a lot of it about.

But as I investigate the possibilities of harnessing my soccer knowledge to wealth, interest wanes. Betting on shirt numbers? Or the number of corners taken during a match? It all sounds far too random rather than a test of skill – and a recipe for losing money rather than making it.

But you know how it is on Google. Especially when you have a book you are supposed to be writing. One click leads to another.

And that's how I come to discover something called *financial spread betting*. It looks hideously complicated. Which makes it a challenge. Everywhere I look, there are warnings that it's a high risk venture. Which tickles my reckless instincts. And somehow, it all seems rather glamorous. Which is appealing on a rainy afternoon in North London.

At this point, a bell goes off in my head, and I start rootling around in the giant-sized Liberty's carrier bag that occupies a corner of my office. This is my Big Bag of Plots. Since I plan to be more than a one-hit wonder as an author, every time I see a newspaper cutting that could become the stuff of fiction, I rip it out and dump it in the bag.

It takes me ten minutes. Then I find it.

The introduction to the piece reads as follows:

"A suburban couple have made huge gains by turning to spread betting instead of investing directly in shares."

The words are accompanied by a picture of a man, who looks disturbingly like John Major, and his blonde accomplice. The pair of them are sporting broad grins. And no wonder. It has taken them just eight weeks to accumulate £1 million by spread betting. It's not a misprint. They really have done it.

"By backing their judgement on MyTravel, British Airways, Skyepharma and others, they are sitting on a handsome profit," the article reports.

I read on. Spread betting, apparently, is the new day trading. Exciting. Frightening. Definitely not for widows and orphans. All you need is a computer and an internet connection.

I have both.

Chapter Three

I am rash, but not stupid

April 2004

One thing was certain. I could never go back to football fixed odds coupons. What was the point?

As some American criminal put it when asked why he robbed banks, "Because that's where the money is." Why waste my time playing for pennies when I could run with the big dogs? Soon, my life savings would be growing instead of shrivelling, and I would be shopping again at Waitrose.

I spend most of my working day at the computer. And because I'm a girlie, I know how to multi-task. What could be simpler than flitting between the screens to keep track of how much I was winning while I bashed away at my novel?

I still hadn't figured out how spread betting worked. To do with share prices, obviously. But think about it. They go up. They go down. How difficult can it be?

"I'm going to be rich," I announce to my dearest friends.

"You've sold your book already? Fantastic! We knew you could do it. How much are they giving you?"

Then the questions get really difficult. After the horrified chorus of "Spread WHAT?" I am asked what it is…how it works…and why on earth would I want to do it?

My answers are, at best, rudimentary.

I am solemnly told it's a dreadful idea…I will lose my shirt, and probably my house as well…I can't possibly succeed at this thing as I'm not Someone in the City…

And my 'evidence' about the people who've become millionaires?

"Sally, you're so gullible! It's one of the things we love most about you. Bet they've lost the lot by now."

"How much?" I snarl.

"How much what?"

"How much do you bet?"

But my dearest friends are not gamblers. They are the ones who read *Jane Eyre* and *Cosmopolitan*. The ones who stayed on for A Levels, while I was invited to swap public school for the local sixth form college.

Later, I ask myself whether my new obsession is really such a good idea.

How much do I know about financial spread betting? As much as I know about Persian pottery or embroidery. (I *can* knit, but don't tell anyone as it would ruin my image.)

I haven't a clue what it's about, but I'm going to do it anyway. I know in my heart that it is only a matter of time. My friends hold down responsible jobs with reputable organisations, but they lack entrepreneurial spirit. Whereas I have been breaking speed limits along the road less travelled since long before I was old enough to drive. I feel quietly superior, although I would never share this thought with my wage-slave contemporaries.

Anyway, I am hearing voices. They come from my computer, and they whisper, "Sally, you are going to be rich."

OK, here comes the rationalisation.

I am Good with Money. Over the years, I've bought and sold various shares – always at a profit – realised endowment mortgages were never going to work, and switched out of them before it was too late, avoided giving any of my cash to institutions like Equitable Life and maintained an impeccably positive bank balance. Moreover, I own a large stained-glass jar that's stuffed full of loose change for a rainy day. My only regret is that I chose a pension rather than a buy-to-let. But, hey, nobody's perfect.

I am rash. But not stupid.

It's time to do my homework.

Chapter Four

I trade my entire knowledge for one cup of coffee

One Week Later

I'm with the latterati at Café 69 in Primrose Hill. Holding court.

"So the marvellous thing about spread betting," I enthuse, "Is that you can make money no matter whether the stock market and individual shares are going up…or down…or even sideways."

"You want another coffee?" offers Retired Reggie. He's a gentleman. And always willing to trade caffeine for useful information.

"But you're telling us you don't actually buy any shares?" Much Married Michael is on the lookout for suggestions that might ease the burden of four sets of alimony.

"That's the beauty of it." There's a big smile on my face. "Spread betting means you can take advantage of stock market moves without owning anything. Not just shares. You can bet on indexes, like the FTSE and the Dow Jones. Or currencies. Gold. Even orange juice futures."

"Like Eddie Murphy in that film where he becomes a Wall Street robber-baron." Retired Reggie is getting excited.

"*Trading Places*, you mean." A movie I saw with my dad. The one where they've stolen the plot of Mark Twain's *The Prince and the Pauper*. "That's right! Murphy makes a fortune on commodities, and now we can, too. Spread betting's a type of derivative, which is a financial instrument that's derived from an underlying market." I notice brows beginning to furrow and eyes starting to glaze, so I cut quickly to the chase. "Take the FTSE Index. Suppose it's trading today at 5000. First question: is it going to go up or down?"

"Up." With his fifth marriage just weeks away, it's hardly surprising that Much Married Michael gravitates instinctively to the sunny side.

"OK, so the first thing you have to do is check the spread. That's the difference between the price of buying and the price of selling – with the actual price falling somewhere in the middle. So with the FTSE at 5000, let's assume the spread is 4998 to 5002. We reckon the FTSE's going up, so that means we buy. How much shall we have?"

"Let's have a tenner," says Retired Reggie. He smacks his wallet on the table and I'm tempted to take his money. Instead, I continue. "OK. We buy at 5002. You always have to buy at the higher price."

Much Married Michael runs an antique shop. He nods his approval at the concept of making customers pay top dollar.

"Let's suppose the FTSE's gone up to 5036, and we decide to sell," I continue. "Every time the index level changes, the spread price changes as well. So now the spread is 5034 to 5038. When you sell, you sell at the lower price." I quell Much Married Michael's inherent protest with a look. "So we bought at 5002 and we've just sold at—"

"5034," they recite.

"Which means?"

Two guys hanging on my every word. It feels great. Maybe I should have been a teacher. "It means we've just captured 32 points of the FTSE – the difference between 5002 and 5034 – and because we went for £10 a point, we've made 32 multiplied by 10. £320."

I have to stop Retired Reggie from ordering champagne. Also, it seems churlish to explain to him that had our imaginary FTSE trade gone the other way, and fallen 32 points, we'd have lost an imaginary £320, which I know is more than he bargained for when he reached for that tenner.

Throughout this exposition, Don the Drug Dealer has hardly said a word. He'd merely grunted when I ask how the cricket spreads were going.

In fact, he's barely spoken to me at all since requesting that I should make it clear he's a pharmaceutical sales representative.

Chapter Five

The meaning of stop-loss and leverage
And an offer I must refuse

One Day Later

"This spread betting thing," says Retired Reggie. We are walking his dog in the park, as we do most mornings. "How long did it take to make the £320?"

"It might have taken half an hour. Or a day. Or a month. That's another thing I like. We're in the driving seat. We can let the trade run until we're ready to take our profit." Or losses. I'm starting to feel guilty that I might be misleading Reggie, so over coffee, I explain the downside.

"I get it," he confirms. "If you bet a tenner on a horse, all you can lose is the tenner. But if your trade goes the wrong way, you can lose your shirt."

Retired Reggie used to be a fashion designer. So I have a go at talking his language. "You can definitely lose the sleeves and the collar. But it's not like Lloyd's, where they take your cufflinks as well. There's something called a stop-loss. You specify the maximum you're prepared to risk on a single trade, and that limits your risk."

"Well at least that means we'll still have enough material to run up a handkerchief and wipe away the tears," he reassures me.

"Or wave the white flag of surrender," adds Much Married Michael.

"But there's also the possibility of winning a jacket and trousers to go with the shirt," continues Retired Reggie. "Which reminds me, young Michael, is it formal attire for your next wedding? If so, I'd better join forces with Sally and do this spread betting business."

The two guys continue their banter, while I mentally go over the concept of leverage. Do I understand it properly? In the corporate world, leverage – or gearing – is the degree to which a company is using borrowed money: the ones that are most highly leveraged are also the ones most likely to go broke because they can't afford to repay their debt.

I don't do debt, so leverage seems instinctively like a bad idea. But according to what I've been reading, for spread betters leverage is actually a good thing. Gives us a big advantage.

In simple English – the sort I prefer – leverage will allow me to turn a small stake into a large profit. The truth is that I still can't explain to myself exactly how it works. Something to do with the fact that because I won't actually own any shares, commodities, or whatever else I trade, I won't have to put up their full value.

What I DO understand is this:

If I buy £10,000 worth of shares, I'll be doing amazingly well if they're worth £12,000 twelve months later. Whereas if I stick

£10,000 in a spread betting account, the rewards could be seriously juicy.

I could easily earn a return of twenty per cent.

Or more.

Much more.

After all, I am Sally Nicoll, former pinball wizard of Portsmouth. Except now I am older and wiser, so I am obliged to remind myself that leverage is a double-edged sword, and I could also lose the lot – and more besides.

But that's just responsible thinking. Lip service to all the *Spread WHAT?* naysayers. Which means everyone I've talked to, except the people currently sitting around this table.

Retired Reggie is gently pulling on my arm. "This spread betting thing," he interrupts my reverie. "I'd love to do it, but at my age, I'm never going to learn how to use a computer."

"And I'm a bit too busy." A wink from Much Married Michael.

"So we want you to do it for us, Sally. How about if we each give you a couple of thousand quid?"

It's a generous offer. And one I could never accept in a million years. To squander my own life savings is one thing. But the thought of Retired Reggie minus his shirt is something else. I have no intention of leveraging his assets.

I shall be putting only my own money where my mouse is.

Chapter Six

Thirteen advantages of spread betting – but only one company for my account

That Afternoon

My novel is not getting written. I've got as far as chapter eight, in which Sir Gerald Akehurst is quarrelling with his lovely, loyal wife. She is beginning to realise he's a nasty piece of work and doesn't deserve her. Maybe she should take her mind off her disintegrating marriage by taking up spread betting instead of all this introspection.

Like Lady Akehurst, I too am looking for distractions. I have spent the past two hours drawing up a list of the advantages of spread betting.

Here it is:

- Sounds really interesting

- Could make me a lot of money

- Will give me a new skill

- Everyone I talk to apart from Reggie and Michael is sceptical.

Such fun to prove them all wrong!

- Can do it while I finish my book

- EVERYTHING I WIN IS TAX FREE!!!! No capital gains or income tax because spread betting currently comes under betting rules

- No messing about with stockbrokers

- No stockbroker commission or brokerage fees

- No share certificates to lose

- No stamp duty to pay, either!

- Can make money when the stock market is falling – or even going sideways – as well as when it's rising

- The stop-loss thingee means I can limit my risk/potential loss on every trade

- Spread betting industry is regulated by the Financial Services Authority, so it can't be that dodgy

I take stock and notice my list has thirteen points. Excellent.

Now it's simply a question of deciding who to open an account with.

There seem to be half a dozen firms to choose from, and I evaluate them all.

Some give the impression of being terribly businesslike and efficient. But they seem intended for City professionals and Donald Trump, rather than me.

I rule out another on the grounds that its website design features such a nasty colour – puce – that I simply can't imagine looking at it on a regular basis.

One company wants me to come to a seminar, but when I deconstruct the invitation, I can see it's a thinly disguised attempt to persuade me to install specialist computer software before I can trade at all.

Then I discover Finspreads.

They explain how spread betting works, and I nod my head as I go through their blurb. Their site is far more user-friendly – and less intimidating – than the rest. Their blue and gold colour scheme is acceptable. They are happy to let me trade in pennies to begin with which means, at the very least, I will be able to lose my money more slowly. They will enrol me into something called the Finspreads Academy, which consists of an eight-week how-to-do-it correspondence course.

And if I go on a recommended beginners course in spread betting, they will stick £100 of FREE MONEY in my account.

It's a no-brainer…

Chapter Seven

An inauspicious start – I am accused of a criminal past

May 2004

Imagine my surprise when the letter comes from Finspreads stating that my application to open an account has been declined.

This is bad enough. But then comes the final sentence of their letter:

"Our decision is final, and will not be reversed."

Now if that's not a challenge, I don't know how to spell incandescent with rage. Or as someone – Liam Gallagher? Bob Geldof? – put it: "Any club that will accept me as a member isn't worth joining."

I know some people might have abandoned spread betting at this stage. But not me!

I take this rejection as a signal that I am destined to get stuck in.

And anyway, as I said earlier, I lead a blameless life – financially, at least – so I'm quietly confident this is merely some tragic clerical error we can all blame on the computer.

I am wrong.

Due to an unfortunate incident involving a neighbour's motorbike, an inefficient insurance broker, a zealous free legal aid specialist, and a wholly innocent victim – by the name of Sally Nicoll – it turns out I have a County Court Judgement against me. For the princely sum of £273.68. Entered, appropriately enough, on 1st April, four years ago.

Oh, the indignity of it all.

And this is the first I've heard about it. Which just goes to show you should never believe a word inefficient insurers say when they tell you everything has been sorted out.

The Finspreads credit control people are very nice about my criminal record (I know, but that's how it feels) and tell me that if I can prove the CCJ is an error, they are sure I will be allowed to open an account after all.

Chapter Eight

I prove my innocence, open my Finspreads account and win something for a rainy day

The Following Saturday

It takes about a week of phone calls and begging letters to procure something called a Certificate of Satisfaction. Which satisfies me. But will this evidence that I am debtworthy – should that be creditworthy? – be enough to satisfy Finspreads?

As it happens, Finspreads is taking part in an Alternative Investments Exhibition, somewhere out in Docklands. I decide to go there in person, armed with proof of my innocence.

I intend to plead my case, that a non-existent debt of £273.68 should not hinder my opportunity to make a fortune out of spread betting.

At the Exhibition, I do my Neville Chamberlain routine. Armed with my precious piece of paper, I confront Finspread's Marketing Director. He is Welsh, but very nice.

He instructs one of his well-dressed minions to issue me with a cup of coffee and a free Finspreads pen, while he himself trots off in search of a photocopying machine.

When he comes back, he assures me there will be no trouble in opening an account. In fact, he's apologising so much, that I begin to feel quite sorry for him.

"I don't know what else we can do to make this up to you," he's saying.

How about a few thousand pounds for my injured feelings, I can't help but think. I despise the compensation culture, but when you're an unpublished author – and not yet a spread betting genius – every little helps.

The Welshman breaks into my avaricious thoughts with a question. "Do you think it will rain today?" he asks.

"No," I reply, ever the optimist.

"Well how about tomorrow?"

"No."

"Or the day after?" The Welshman is becoming quite intense, and I'm wondering if this is some sort of trading test. Perhaps he wants to see if I can keep my nerve under pressure.

"I expect it will rain some time in the next month." I avoid eye contact and keep my tone matter-of-fact.

At last, I have arrived at the correct answer.

Which is how I come to be in possession of a splendid blue-and-white Finspreads umbrella, which was thrust into my hands with a gesture of great relief.

Oh, and I also own a freshly-opened Finspreads account.

Chapter Nine

The Welshman invites me to write about my new life as a novice spread better

Tuesday

The latterati is in Emergency Session.

"So you guys are saying I should do it?" I look uncertainly at Retired Reggie and Much Married Michael. I'm even too agitated to notice that Jude Law is sitting in the corner of our cafe where he feeds wholewheat toast to his son.

"Course you should," declares Reggie. "Don't understand why you're hesitating."

"For a start, I haven't really got a clue about spread betting. So I can't imagine why on earth anyone would want to read what I say."

"But you're writing a novel, " Reggie counters. "And you've never done that before. How's it going, by the way?"

Before I can change the subject, Much Married Michael – sun-bronzed in the aftermath of his latest nuptials – tears himself away from the Welshman's letter. "Look here," he says. "These people at Finspreads are actually offering to pay you for writing a blog about spread betting. They must be mad, but that's a different issue. What's the difference between writing about spread betting on their website and writing about assassinations, conspiracies and Alzheimer's disease?" Michael took my partially-completed manuscript with him on honeymoon, and I'm touched that he's found time to read it. Or is that a sign that the marriage is in trouble already?

Don the Drug Dealer – sorry, pharmaceutical sales executive – is back on speaking terms with me, and he's equally encouraging. "Go for it, Sally!" he declares. "Gift horses, mouths and all that. And if there's money involved, you're getting *paid* to do something you want to do anyway. What part of lucky git don't you understand?"

But still I hesitate. I would feel like a fraud. Diarists are people like Samuel Pepys and Adrian Mole, not me. I see myself more as a Frederick Forsyth, Ken Follett or Robert Ludlum (but don't get alarmed; I look nothing like any of them).

What I know about spread betting might be a little bit more than the public at large. But not much more. The Welshman reckons Finspreads customers will enjoy reading about the experiences of a fellow trader. But I'm concerned I'll be setting myself up for ridicule, like a contestant on Big Brother.

And then I look into Retired Reggie's watery blue eyes, and I'm reminded of my dad. If only he'd lived to see the day. His little Sally. Writing about gambling. And getting paid for writing about gambling. He'd have been the proudest man in Portsmouth.

Perhaps it might even be fun to record my progress. Will I fall at the first fence? Or am I destined to own a yacht and a small Mediterranean island?

So now I am a Novice Spread Better. Official.

When I get back from Café 69, I write a quick letter to my Great Uncle Gareth. The Taffia, I realise, is everywhere: even in my own address book. My scribble is actually a shamefully overdue thank you for the Christmas present he sent me. I write in encouraging terms about my novel (another day has passed without me adding to the manuscript) and with almost-genuine enthusiasm about my new job as a spread betting columnist. I know he'll be chuffed, because he shares the family love of gambling.

A love, I should add, that is definitely not shared by my mum or my Big Brother. So far as they are concerned, escapades on the race course or in the betting shop are the love that dare not speak its name. And as for spread betting…

… if they knew what it was, and that I am about to do it, they'd be horrified.

So I decide not to tell them.

Chapter Ten

Mr. Big's Top Ten Tips
And why you should
never be kind to your mother

Friday 7th May

Here I am, the Carrie Bradshaw of spread betting.

And still a virgin.

I want my first time to be special. I want to be sure I know what I'm doing. And even though I am under no illusions about getting it right every time, I want my first trade to be a winner.

Are my three wishes realistic?

Francis Bacon – or more likely Max Clifford – said:

"Knowledge is power"

So it seems like a good idea to get myself clued up before finally getting stuck in.

This is how I come to be sitting in a room somewhere north of Peterborough surrounded by fourteen men. Two are pretty fit. But I only have eyes for the one who stands at the front of the class.

My Mr Big is called John Bartlett, and his version of whispered sweet nothings is:

"Stick with me and I'll show you how to trade with confidence."

I had found John by following the links on the Finspreads web site; the ones that promised to pay £100 into my account if I agreed to spend double that on a one-day beginners' course in spread betting.

Unlike some of the self-styled financial gurus I've investigated online, men who are promising me overnight wealth just as soon as I write them a fat cheque, I can look at John without mentally rearranging the words oil, salesman and snake. His lack of a suit makes it look like he's on 'our' side, rather than the City's side. And the moment he opens his mouth, he has my full attention.

"I used to bet on the horses," he tells us. "And then I discovered that every afternoon at 2.30 sharp, there's this race that takes place in America. It's called the Dow Jones Stakes and it runs for six-and-a-half-hours. Basically, it's a two-horse race, and you can bet to win, or if you think there's going to be a slip-up, you can bet to lose. You don't have to put your money on before the race begins. In fact, you can wait until one side's well ahead and then make up your mind. Oh, and you can claim your winnings any time you happen to be ahead. I can't remember the last time I backed a horse."

Trading, John tells us, is a zero sum game: the winners' winnings are the losers' losses. Our fellow-traders are not so much colleagues, as opponents.

I am still absorbing this statement during the coffee break when I begin exchanging pleasantries with another participant. He's already begun trading and lost £300 on a single trade, apparently because he had to take his 84-year-old mother to the shops, and by the time she'd bought her rice pudding and Marmite, the market had fallen faster than the price of McDonald's next time there's an outbreak of BSE. (See, John has taught me to think like a trader.)

I know it is uncharitable, and I will probably burn in hell even for thinking it, but I say a little prayer: "Please may I have this man who is so kind to his mother as my opponent."

Back behind our desks, I take notes. Here are 10 useful things I learned today:

1 We can be wrong 50% of the time and still make a profit. (Just like GCSEs, where mostly incorrect answers can still earn you an A*.)

2 Most traders go bust within the first nine months. (Not us, hopefully; we're here to learn how to stay in the game.)

3 Most traders fail because they overtrade. They place bets left, right and centre, instead of waiting for a decent opportunity. (Unlikely in my case; I feel too scared even to make my first trade.)

4 Success is 70% to 90% about money management, rather than the markets we choose to trade. (This gives me hope, as I'm good at budgeting.)

5 Technical analysis – where you study graphs of share price movements – can be useful because patterns tend to repeat themselves. (Until today, my interest in charts was confined to

horoscopes – I am a Virgo – but John has been explaining how we can analyse charts in order to predict where the market will go next.)

6 Markets tend to fall three times faster than they rise. (Interesting, but I still have to get my head around the fact that you can make money by selling – going short, they call it – and then buying back at a lower price. Especially as you don't own anything.)

7 Always trade with a stop-loss. That's where you specify the absolute maximum you're prepared to risk on any particular trade, (John repeats this many times during the day, so I guess it's important.)

8 Plan your trades. Trade your plan. (Excellent, as a Virgo, I just love planning ahead and making numbered lists.)

9 Volume tells the story. (Comedy? Tragedy? Thriller?)

10 Avoid trading during the first 30 minutes of the day. (Good news, as I don't want anything to interfere with my coffee-drinking routine.)

"Of course," says John Bartlett, "it's one thing to give people a set of do's and don'ts. And I know you're all sitting here thinking you're going to follow my excellent advice to the letter." An ironic sigh. "But you won't. Believe me, you won't."

I prepare to leave the course with a fistful of hand-outs that will remind me what I've learned along with various financial and trading web site recommendations. And with John's final words ringing in my ears.

"When you trade, you begin to find out who you really are. How you handle pressure. How you cope with failure. And how you deal with success. You will find your own style. Some of you will make dozens of trades in a week. Others might make only two or three in a fortnight. Some of you will get disillusioned and give up. Others will forget what's been said today, lose money and give up. And someone here might turn out to be a big success."

I notice that the Man Who Is Kind To His Mother is sitting up straight, with a steely resolve in his eye. Maybe I'll choose someone else as my opponent.

Back home again, and on the verge of my very first trade.

The moment of truth is approaching.

Chapter Eleven

My first trades reveal if I am a chicken or a pig

Three days Later

Believe in your ability to be a pig.

This sounds like something out of a fortune cookie. Yet there it sits in the subject line of a message that's dropped into the inbox of my newly opened email account: veryluckymoney@hotmail.com.

What does it mean?

For a start, it means Finspreads has announced my debut as an online diarist. And it's evidence that people are reading the stuff.

It turns out I have a message from George K, who begins by telling me, "I am now into my third month of trading with Finspreads, and I know the true meaning of Greed and Fear."

Eagerly, I read on.

George has sent me an entertaining little parable about a chicken and a pig who decide to go into business together. They consider their assets, and decide to start a bacon and egg bar.

"Now the chicken was interested in the business. But the pig – well he was thoroughly committed. Or to put it another way," says George, just in case I haven't got it, "The only genuine way to test yourself is to do it for real."

The time has definitely come to dip a trotter in the water if not the full rasher.

Remembering what I learned at John Bartlett's Trading Seminar, I draw up my trading plan. It goes like this:

I shall sit at my computer and make a series of small trades so I can experience the Finspreads trading platform in action. The maximum I am prepared to lose is 1% of my starting balance, which works out at £50.

The swift – and numerate – amongst you will have calculated that my Finspreads account was therefore £5000 in credit. No donations from Retired Reggie or Much Married Michael. Gambling with other people's money would place me under far too much pressure to succeed, although I'm still touched by my chums' blind faith.

You're probably thinking £5k is a lot of money. Correct. But as I say, I've earned well over the years, and I've always stashed regular sums into a savings account. Interest rates are rubbish at the moment, so I've allocated a lump sum in pursuit of success in spread betting. It's like investing in a new hobby. I've decided against starting small and then feeling depressed when my beginner mistakes and duff trades make the account even smaller. By lobbing in £5k, I'm giving myself enough of a starting bank to take spread betting seriously. If and when my balance is down to zero, too bad.

There's no benevolent dad to bale me out if it all goes wrong. But rest assured, I've followed his Golden Rule. Even if I lose the lot, I won't be ruined. Egg on my face, for sure – the thought makes me refocus on George's chicken – but if I screw up I'll just have to shop at Kwik Save and get some advertising work sooner rather than later. Unpleasant, but not the end of the world. You never bet more than you can afford to lose. Never.

Anyway. I've logged onto the Finspreads trading platform. Basically, it reminds me of the souk I visited in Istanbul: frantic buying and selling everywhere you look, although since this is a cyberspace bazaar, there's no throb of conversation or selection of interesting aromas. Like the real-life equivalent, you can trade in gold, silver and foodstuffs. But there's other stuff, too.

Tons of other stuff.

Let's start with the London Stock Exchange – if only for the reason that its original home was Jonathan's Coffee-House, and I'm on my fifth cup of Douwe Egberts, even though it's not even mid-morning. The FTSE 100 Index, barometer of the British economy, has opened the week lower, I notice, and is currently trading at 4450.

Moving on…

- I can trade any of the stocks that belong to the Index. These are the blue chips that we've all heard of: names like Abbey National, British Airways, Reuters and so forth.

- Or I can drop a division and trade in the fortunes of companies that are listed on the FTSE 250 (smaller companies like Burberry and easyJet).

- No passport necessary to trade a bunch of European stocks from the exchanges of Germany, Holland, Italy, Spain, France and Switzerland (this could be my chance to bet on the company that makes Louis Vuitton bags).

- A few more mouse clicks and I'm on virtual Wall Street. Here in America, I can trade their main indexes – the Dow, S&P and NASDAQ – as well as what looks like about 500 individual shares.

- There are also separate parts of the site where I can go to trade currencies, commodities, interest rates and bonds. (Eat your heart out Eddie Murphy, OJ futures here I come).

Confused yet?

I am! And then I notice something else. Say I decide to punt on British Airways. I can trade something that says British Airways Rolling (unwise for a 747, surely) or British Airways June, British Airways September, or indeed British Airways December.

Is this the same as Coke, Diet Cola and Vanilla Coke – diversification of the product line?

Or what?

I retreat to my notes from the Finspreads Academy to figure it out.

Turns out it's all to do with how long you reckon your trade will last. The Rolling Shares are best for short-term trades. They have the tightest spreads – the gap between the sell and buy prices, I remind myself – and the reason they are called Rolling is because if you leave your trade open, Finspreads rolls it over, and it remains in play, day after day, until you close it, or it hits your stop-loss.

Anything with a month after its name – British Airways SEPTEMBER – comes under the heading of a Share Futures contract. These are best for longer-term trades. You can keep them open as long as you want, up until the expiry date, when your trade is automatically cancelled. The contract that's due to expire last has the widest spread, so you'd only choose it if you were planning to let your trade run and run.

Stands to reason that a futures contract for, say, September, expires at the end of the month of September.

Right?

Wrong.

Expiry day can come at any time during the month. I make a mental note to ensure I don't get caught out by an unexpected sell-by date. Which would seem especially easy in the metals bazaar, where the June expiry dates happen in May!

Enough of this window shopping. I realise it doesn't really matter what I trade, the important thing is to get it over and done with.

Time to wake up and smell the bacon.

I'm hoping to sell my novel in America, so I advance towards the currencies section of the website. I'm going to trade on the rate of exchange between the dollar and the pound. Mr Big had mentioned that the professionals refer to this as "trading Cable". I wonder why, and consult Google to discover the answer. The search engine's top hits assure me it's got something to do with Jim Carrey, but I'm not convinced.

Deeper probing reveals the answer: it's because of the first underground cable across the Atlantic that linked the UK with the USA. That's interesting, I wonder…

But I have procrastinated long enough.

- I go to where the market description says IMM British Pound (£/$) June. There's an eight point spread.

- I declare that I am going to bet 1p per point, then my cursor hits the button marked TRADE.

- A decisive stab of the mouse.

- A sudden flash of blue arrows circle the globe as the Finspreads site goes to work to quote me a price.

- The price appears and I click again, on the SELL button.

- My first trade is up and running.

And the whole process has taken less than ten seconds.

My eyes stare unblinking at the screen. Cable's as active as a baby in the womb. And today, it's kicking the right way for me. The trade's going in my favour.

Moments pass and I'm 18 points ahead – or ten points when you include the spread. A couple of clicks later, and I'm out of the trade. Phew!

I have started with a winner, and my account is swollen by ten pence.

I do a little victory dance and wonder if Warren Buffet experiences similar pleasure when he gets it correct. (He reckons, incidentally, that derivatives are financial weapons of mass destruction, posing a threat to the entire economic system, so I guess he's not a

Finspreads customer.) Just think, if my stake had been higher: A £1 trade would have made me a tenner. And if I'd bet £10, I'd be £100 in profit within the space of a minute. Advertising paid well, but never that well.

What FUN!

Clearly, I have mastered Greed.

Within the next hour I have developed my first original trading theory.

Sally Nicoll's Trading Theory #1:

> *Spread betting is like serial killing – the more frequently you do it, the easier it becomes.*

Soon, I am clicking merrily away, opening trades faster than you can say, "Stop pressing these buttons. Think about what you're doing. You're meant to buy instead of sell there, but you hit the wrong key."

It's as if someone's given me the freedom of Prada at Matalan prices. My basket overflows with FTSE Futures, FTSE Cash, laced with another bite of Cable – I obviously took my winnings too soon – plus a dash of Gas & Oil, topped with a smattering of Gold. All at a penny a trade, and without any need to go foot-slogging around the bazaar.

Up and down I skip along the trading aisles, picking indiscriminately, until something really does take my fancy: it's called MIB, Daily Cash, Friday. Whatever that might be.

I'm interested because I've learned that volatility is good for trading.

In other words, my prey needs to shift its price one way or another – and ideally, the way I've decided it's going to go, in order to rack up the points.

Right now, this MIB thingee is way down on the day, but I'm sure it's going to bounce back up.

Forty minutes later and it's lunchtime. I now have eight positions and a little row of minuses against each and every one of them, reminding me of my school reports. This is no longer going according to plan – not my plans of avarice, at any rate – as I am losing £1.53 overall. The only bright note is that the MIB, which sank like a stone from the instant I pressed BUY, is recovering a bit.

On the principle that a watched pot never boils, I do what any sensible trader would do. Put the computer in sleep mode and go out to buy a new mobile phone.

One thing leads to another, and I get back to my trades three hours later to discover it hasn't got any better. I take a deep breath and swallow my position on Cable. There goes £1.16 of the Nicoll Life Savings.

As for the MIB. I've discovered it's Italy's answer to the FTSE. I decide it's like an Italian boyfriend I once had. Filthy Lucca. Intriguing. Beguiling. Unpredictable. Seductive. Yet ultimately far too unreliable for me. I close my MIB trade for a loss of £3.39.

I've been told that it can be hard to cut your losses. Admit you were wrong. Maybe this is a Boy Thing? I decide to simplify matters, and cut a few more positions without any particular feelings of heartbreak.

Then I turn my attention to the Dow Jones.

I go to Yahoo Finance and I start looking at the chart, which is free and in real time. Yes, I know I should have been chart watching a lot earlier in the day, but hey, I'm only splashing in the shallows here. More chicken than pig.

It seems, though, that my talent for technical analysis is matched only by my ability to map read. Either that, or I have a spooky power to turn the markets the other way, the moment I place a trade. More losing trades follow.

There is however, one bright moment. Remember Gas & Oil? I'm up 45 points! Shall I cash in, or ride my luck?

While I am deciding, my screen tells me the price is 'indicative', and I must phone to trade. Nice as they are at Finspreads, I don't have the gall to call to ask if I can close a 1p trade. My mistake, because by the time I am able to do the job myself, I discover I've lost 7p.

Is there a person at Finspreads, watching my bets and making them lose? Maybe it's the Welshman. Paranoia is setting in. And my eyes ache. Time to call it a day.

I have completed 18 trades. Twelve losers. One break-even. Four winners. Overall, I am £7.27p down. But at least I've stuck to my plan and learned how to operate the Finspreads trading platform.

I am a pig with a slightly subdued oink.

Chapter Twelve

Random trading for less than the minimum wage

The Third Week of May

How did we ever manage before email? It's so easy to complain to Camden Council about the disgraceful activities of their so-called Street Wardens who patrol Regents Park Road and tell us we're obstructing the pavement, when all we want is to enjoy a cup of coffee in the fresh air.

"Go on then. Arrest me!" challenged Retired Reggie, when the jumped-up uniform solemnly informed him he was sitting six inches outside the official area – marked with studs – where we're allowed to put our chairs.

We call these guys the Stud Nazis. A fact I mentioned yesterday, when I emailed the council to complain about their harassment of my elderly pal.

Now I am in receipt of an email from a council apparatchik, who tells me he is 'personally offended' by my use of the word Nazi.

I respond by telling him my grandmother was a refugee from Hitler's Germany, and that I have a genetic fear of being confined within a designated space.

I wonder if I will be allowed to continue trading once Camden has me locked up for Assault with a Dangerous Vocabulary.

While I'm deleting the word fuckwit from the final line of my reply, fresh email arrives.

The latest message is from someone called Richard F and it's typical of several I've received since I wrote online about my first experience of trading.

"727 points down?" it goes, "I feel quite humble. I shall never feel the same about being 20 points down again. Thanks for the tonic, I feel much better!"

Richard observes that if I'd been trading at £25 a point, I'd have lost £18,175 on my debut afternoon.

Meanwhile, my dearest friends, convinced I shouldn't be trading at all, have been repeating, "Told you so!" ever since I reported on my first adventure.

Even Reggie and Michael are telling me not to get carried away. "If you lose your money too fast, you'll have nothing to write about," Much Married Michael is ever the pragmatist.

But everyone's missing something important.

Had I been trading £25 a point – fat chance – there's no way I'd have been using last week's suck-it-and-see strategy. The strength of the Finspreads approach is that it enables a complete beginner like me to learn, without risking anything like serious money. I've got another seven weeks of being able to trade at 1p a point – experimenting with what works and what doesn't – and I intend to make the most of it.

Not that I've been trading every day. Guilt has driven me back to my novel. It's going well; another 15,000 words added. I don't know how much you know about writers, but generally speaking, we fall into two camps: those who begin by writing an outline of their story, with all the plot twists mapped out, and those who go wherever the words take them. As a Virgo, I am an outliner. Naturally. But no matter how carefully I plan, there's always a surprise when I flesh out my chapter skeletons. The latest surprise being that chapter eleven contains half of chapter twelve.

That puts me nicely ahead of the game, so I feel entitled to log back into my Finspreads account.

Surprise!

I am losing £1.63. So that's another lesson I hope I've learned: those Rolling thingees that are meant to be for short-term trades continue to rock – with winnings or losses added or taken from your account every day – even when you've forgotten all about them!

It's not entirely a disaster, though. Last time I traded, I switched from selling to buying Cable. That trade has remained open, too, and now I'm winning £2.97 for a stake of 3p. (A quick bit of maths: this means that in real life, the rate of exchange has dropped by 297 divided by three: 99cents. Just thought you might like to know.)

Cool!

I decide to quit while I'm ahead. But in my enthusiastic greed, I stab the wrong button, and discover I've increased my stake, instead of cashing in. I've been so inept that I now have two separate 3p sell trades in play. Three hours later, and I'm 39p down on the newer trades, and my original winnings are diminishing, as well. So I cash in on my profits from the original Cable trade, while persevering with the losing position.

By the end of the day, thanks to my incorrect predictions about the Dow's recovery and another currency trade involving the movement of sterling against the Swiss franc, my remaining trades are down £4.84.

At which point, I decide to give up, grab a coffee and see if the Stud Nazis are waiting to arrest me.

"You've just missed them," says Retired Reggie. "How's it going, girl?"

But I sense the question is rhetorical, and one look at Much Married Michael tells me I have interrupted a serious conversation. "What's up?" I ask.

"There's good news. And bad news."

Since when did Reggie become Michael's PR man?

"What's the good news?"

"Michael's getting a dog."

"And the bad?" Somehow I already know the answer, and a glance at Michael's hand, around his coffee cup, confirms my suspicions. There it is, the revealing white circle on his naked, suntanned finger. "What happened?"

"It wasn't my fault." At least Michael has recovered the power of speech. "How was I supposed to know that Caro and Holly go to the same hairdresser?"

He's referring to wives Three and Five.

"And?"

"They were there at the same time. They started talking to one another."

They would, wouldn't they. In some parts of the world, two ex-wives would pull out one another's hair by way of a greeting. But here in Primrose Hill we do something far more dangerous for the men in our lives. We engage in conversation.

"And?"

"It was the honeymoon."

Michael sounds as if he took his latest bride to Dracula's castle, but I know better. "You said you had a great time. Gondolas at sunset. Private beach and swimming pool. Limo tour of the glass factories." Michael's had a lot of practice at honeymoons and knows how to do them well. I'd been jealous.

"Holly found out I took Caro to Venice, and—"

"Then she found out he took Wendy, Lisa and Simone there, too, " sighs Reggie. "Same hotel. Same gondola. Same everything except the dates."

"Why change a winning formula?"

But Michael's protest fails to convince even him.

"So what kind of a dog are you getting?" I try to lift the mood.

The Tibetan terrier will be arriving next week.

I spend the following day shopping for puppy stuff with Much Married Michael and getting to grips with my next chapter. The manuscript pages are starting to stack up nicely. Either I am creating a damn good story, or a big pile of words.

Thirty-six hours pass before I return to my Finspreads account. And this time, the benign neglect has paid off. Each of my remaining trades are moving in the correct direction. Even that hit-the-wrong-button Cable trade has shifted 131 points into the black, and my combined profits come to 235 points.

So maybe the thing to do is to hold your nerve when you're losing? And I wonder whether to share this insight with Michael, but realise how much easier it is to handle loss when you're playing for pennies instead of pounds – or hearts.

For the rest of the week, I continue to monitor my existing trades and resist the temptation to place any new ones. Everything's moving in the right direction – even though my selections have been entirely haphazard – and now I know what Michael and Don the pharma sales executive mean when they laugh about how much pleasure they get from their computers.

I'm making £2.37 from a 3p buy trade on the Dow Jones. But just as I'm congratulating myself, Wall Street takes a tumble, and most of my winnings vanish before you can say, "Refresh your browser in case it's a mistake."

Which brings us to Friday. Expiry date for the May Dow Futures thingee. I've decided to sweat it out to the bitter end, hoping the Index goes up, so my profits reappear.

Meanwhile, I have devised a cunning plan

Sally Nicoll's Cunning Plan #1:

> *What if I also back the Daily Dow to fall, by selling at 5p a point? I think this is what they mean by hedging – and whatever happens to the American stock market, I'll end up in profit.*

But even as I make the trade, I wonder if I'm digging a big hole for myself. Thanks to some judicious hand-eye coordination, I manage to take 15 points – 75p – when the Dow continues to fall. And I flog off my remaining Cable for a profit of 154 points.

Oh, and I had better own up to my foolish bet on Yahoo Rolling; I had noticed the company was due for an announcement on Friday and the price had risen steeply so I backed it to fall, just on a hunch. That cost me 57 points, although it could have been even worse – it was up 97 points at one stage during the session.

By the end of Week Two of my career as a trader I have won 460 points and lost 178, for a total profit of £5.53.

That night, I share my success with my dearest friends.

"And just how much is the minimum wage these days?" they smirk.

Chapter Thirteen

Commonsense spread betting wins me pretty new underwear and two free tanks of petrol

June

The Welshman forwards me an email.

"I've been following the episodes of Sally Nicoll's Diary," it begins. "Where's the next chapter? Did she sell when she should have bought? Or vice versa? And was she in for £10 a point rather than 10p, and consequently her laptop, went flying out of her top floor flat window? Cheers, Mike K."

Don't worry, Mike. I live in a basement. And while you are partially correct – I've started playing for higher stakes – the news is good. I've been winning!

In fact, I've made a net profit of £138.45 since placing my first trade. That's a 2.7% return on my £5000 starting bank. Infinitely superior to the amount of interest I'd have received if the cash had stayed tucked away in the savings account for another month.

I know I should be reporting that I've achieved this after careful study of chart patterns. I'm meant to be able to identify:

- *Double tops*
  This doesn't mean you've scored 40 playing darts. It's when you look at the chart and see what looks like two mountain peaks. Or the price moving in a pattern like the letter M. This means the price is likely to fall. Apparently.

- *Double bottoms*
  Nothing to do with our obesity epidemic. They're the opposite of double tops. So either you spot them by standing on your head, or you're looking for a letter W. The signal that the price is about to go up. Allegedly.

- *Head and shoulders*
  Not the shampoo to banish dandruff. If you peer carefully at the chart you can see little dips for the shoulders and a bigger dip for the neck. Again, it means the price is on the rise. And no, I am not making this up.

There's lots more.

You're meant to be able to spot flags, pennants and various types of triangles – and they're all pointers to the market's next move. But I'm as good at technical analysis as I am at speaking Mandarin Chinese.

The truth is that my recent successes are down to common sense, pure and simple.

First of all, Marks and Spencer. You remember, Philip Green offered over £8 billion to buy them. I missed the immediate quantum leap in the share price when he made his move. But come the next morning, I was glued to his coat-tails. It seemed like the right moment to play for a meaningful stake, so I made my first significant spread bet: I bought Marks and Spencer for £5 a point.

Then I watched the price go up.

At this point, I adjusted my stop-loss to make sure that whatever happened, I'd still make a profit. (You do this by fixing it above the price at which you originally bought.) Sure enough, as the price began to fall, my stop-loss got hit. I'd made £15.50 – enough for some Per Una bloomers.

But it could have been better.

Like most new spread betters, I'd taken my winnings too soon.

So I went back into the Marks and Spencer share price, and this time I stayed in until Friday afternoon, when suddenly the price began ticking up. I cashed in for £31, feeling extremely smug. Not only did the price go right back down within seconds, but now I have the matching bra, as well.

My other common sense trade was even more profitable.

This week, my dearest friends have been getting agitated about the price of petrol. While they've been moaning, I've been hitting the buy button on Brent Crude Oil. I exercised some caution, as oil is a more volatile market – the price tends to dance about a lot during the course of every trading session, so you can lose money quickly, although, of course, that is not the intention. I confined myself to a 50p a point trade. Result? A gain of £18.50 in the time it took me to read two identical email circulars suggesting we all boycott Shell and BP, and another that wanted me to write to Gordon Brown about fuel duty.

Instead of writing to the Chancellor, I turned to CNN and saw an item about OPEC meeting to discuss their output figures. The tone of the item was sufficiently reassuring to prompt me to place a £1 sell bet. Sure enough, the market behaved as I hoped, and I scooped another £67 out of cyberspace.

Mind you, my wins are small beer compared to some. According to an item in *The Sunday Times*, a bloke who started off with £27,000 in his spread betting account has doubled his money in the past few weeks by trading exclusively in oil futures – and he's quoted as saying that until recently he didn't know anything about them.

Good for him. As for me, not only do I have clean underwear to celebrate my first decent winning trade, I can also afford to fill my tank twice over.

See, I told you this was going to be fun.

Chapter Fourteen

How my next spread bet is prompted by a Japanese fighting dog

A Few Days Later

Much Divorced Michael's new life partner has arrived. And what a surprise package she's turned out to be.

"If that dog's a Tibetan terrier, I'll buy a computer and learn how to do this spread betting thing myself!" Retired Reggie is adamant that Michael's been sold a pup.

We all troop off to Primrose Hill Books to see if we can identify what breed the dog is. Marek, the proprietor, won't let us across the threshold. "Look at the sign!" he insists, and points out the notice in his shop window that decrees: "No dogs admitted apart from guide dogs." I've always thought this is weird, especially since I've never come across a Braille section. Presumably the only guide dogs who do cross the threshold are those who've overshot Primrose Hill Pets, which is next door.

We emerge from the bookshop with an illustrated volume called

World Dogs and stand in the street, ruling out possibilities. Reggie's right. If this is a Tibetan terrier, something's definitely been lost in translation. Yorkie, Staffie, Spaniel and German Shepherd are also swiftly eliminated.

Then along comes Elaine, who's in charge of the pet shop. "Ahh," she coos. "You don't see many of these around!" She calls her colleagues, Charlene and Becky, and they all enthuse over the sullen ball of fur as if it's a new-born baby.

"You know what it is?" Michael sounds relieved.

"Course we do!" Charlene is authoritative. "She's definitely got some Japanese Tosa in her. Great guard dogs. I think they're Japan's equivalent of pit bulls, so she may grow up to be a bit on the boisterous side. Might be a bit of Doberman there, as well. Isn't she beautiful!"

Reggie and I have named the puppy Tossa. And now Michael's in a huff because he thinks we're referring to him.

I return home, having cheerfully wasted most of the morning, to the latest batch of emails from my Finspreads fan club. There's one that's just serendipadocious.

"Hi Sally," begins Richard H. "Have you looked at the Sep £/yen?"

Um, no. When it comes to currency trading, I've experimented with nothing more exotic than sterling and the dollar.

"The Japanese economy is just coming out of a period of deflation," continues Richard H. "The Bank of Japan is not going to put up interest rates – their recovery is largely export-led, and they will not want the yen to appreciate much, so if the spot price doesn't change you make a tidy profit."

I understand some of this: not the bit about spot prices, but the word profit seems pretty unambiguous. The message seems seriously authoritative. And now a Japanese killer puppy has entered my life. It must be a sign!

I leap in and buy for £1.

Next time I check the market, I'm losing £144.

Was Richard H having a laugh? I take another look at his message. "The other good thing about this market is the high volatility, which is good for trades with quite a big bid/offer spread."

Bid/offer spreads I understand: with Finspreads, that's the difference between the sell price and the buy price. But high volatility doesn't seem so good when you're on the wrong end of it.

I email Richard H. "Um, where should I place the stop-loss?" He's online, which makes for an immediate answer. "I don't use stops. My Finspreads trades are small compared to my overall investment portfolio."

Not especially helpful. I check my account. Now I'm only losing £110.

"Would you be worried if you were losing £1.10p?" I ask myself. Remembering how sanguine I was when my penny trades were down 110 points, I leave well alone.

A good move, since the rate of exchange between sterling and yen is well volatile. Over the past few days, the price has been up and down like the zip on Filthy Lucca's chinos. (He's the sexiest boyfriend I ever had, and I still miss him.) At one point, I was £40 or so in profit, and at the time of writing, I'm £5 down. I plan to take profits if and when I get at least £60 ahead.

And I'll buy Tossa some teething rings to celebrate.

But not before I select some equities I can trade longer-term, with September contracts.

I nip out to the newsagents and come back with a copy of the FT. Their football coverage is rubbish. I spend an hour going through the other bits of the paper and then place five new trades:

- £5 BUY Smith & Nephew at 583.6

- £1 BUY AstraZeneca at 2604.7 (it seems too volatile to risk £5 a point)

- £5 BUY JJB Sports at 271.4

- £5 SELL Berkeley Group at 888.5

- £5 SELL easyJet at 162.7

Spread betting is less complicated than I thought. All it takes is practice.

Chapter Fifteen

In which I almost make £900 – but it all goes horribly wrong

The Following Friday

I was so looking forward to telling you how I only just failed to make £900 in three hours.

Instead, I am obliged to share with you the story of how I was sucked into my first major disaster.

Remember that sell bet on the Berkeley Group? (Incidentally, sell bets are also known as 'going short'.) My trade was placed at 888.5 and I was expecting the price to fall. When that happened, I'd be able to buy them back for less than I'd paid, which would put me into profit. So yes – in response to a few emails I've received lately from my growing band of Finspreads readers – with spread betting you can make money when the share price of a company goes down, even though you don't own any of their shares in the first place.

I'd decided Berkeley was ripe for plucking for the following reasons:

- interest rates are rising

- that means mortgages will be more expensive

- which spells doom and gloom in the housing market

- and bad times for builders

- Berkeley is already trending down (their chart shows that generally speaking their share price is falling)

- and their annual profits statement is due soon.

This week, the Berkeley share price has defied its trend, and climbed steadily, but not significantly, higher. By last night I was about 30 points – or £150 – down, but still confident that if I held tight, I'd be able to close my trade in profit.

Today, I logged into my Finspreads account just before lunchtime. This is later than usual – a good thing, since it spared me several additional hours of pain.

I am sure that like most customers, the first thing I always notice once my account details appear is the 'Open Profit & Loss' figure. This tells me the current value of my open trades.

I couldn't believe my eyes.

There was a minus sign next to £1,463.

Naturally, I thought there was something wrong with the trading system. Some glitch in their computers.

Alas, no.

Evidently, the bloody Berkeley Group agrees with me that the property market looks dodgy. Indeed, they have issued a statement saying they plan to abandon house building and focus on urban regeneration instead.

This tragic piece of news has skyscrapered the share price. The company value increased by twenty-eight per cent in a matter of minutes. Leaving me in big, BIG, trouble.

"But what about your stop-loss?" I hear you seasoned, sensible traders cry.

The simple truth is that I didn't have one. I hadn't seen the need. The UK equities market is nowhere near as volatile, as, say, my old adversary the MIB index. And even if I had taken the precaution, I wouldn't have guaranteed it (this is where you pay extra to be absolutely sure you don't pay a penny more than the amount you've specified you're willing to risk on the trade), so I'd still have taken the hit when the share price gapped upward.

I just lost twenty-nine per cent of my trading bank.

Be calm, Sally. Deep breaths.

TWENTY-NINE PER CENT!

Not so much a shirt as the whole damn wardrobe.

I'm gutted.

I'm trying very hard to be philosophical, though. At the risk of sounding like David Beckham, I reckon I was simply a bit unlucky, and I'm still up to the job of spread betting.

It's pretty rare for a UK share to leap 267 points in a single session. There's a clear reason why it happened, and I couldn't possibly have known in advance. So I'm putting it down to experience as an Act of God, and continuing my adventure just a little more cautiously.

Besides, as well as disaster, there have also been triumphs. My long trade on Smith & Nephew has made me £48. The JJB Sport punt ended in a £20 profit (I sold with thanks to Marcus H, who told me their Balham High Road branch was deserted) and easyJet's decline made me enough to fly to Paris, with Ryanair.

Small, steady profits like this will do me fine.

And you certainly didn't hear me complain when Cairn Energy (tipped by the *The Mail on Sunday* as a momentum stock) made me £295 for a £2 buy bet in the space of 48 hours. Or when I noticed on the 'losers' section of Yahoo Finance that Filtronic was taking a beating; I sold for £2 and emerged £58 better off over three days.

But what about that £900 I failed to win?

I'm learning to think twice before accepting tips from people who read my Finspreads blog, however well intentioned they might be.

You remember. That trade I made on sterling/yen. (Tossa has put on three pounds this week, incidentally.) It's all been going badly, and I've been carrying a loss. The way I see it, you only lose real money when you close the trade; up until then, it's only a paper loss. But on this one, I finally reckoned I was beaten.

Enter a new plan.

Sally Nicoll's Cunning Plan #2:

> *Instead of watching my losses mount, I will change horses in mid-stream. I will take my losses on the chin and then sell the*

currency, instead of buying it.

So I hit the sell button. And then a funny thing happens – although it seems anything but amusing at the time.

To my horror, I now have a £9 sell trade in place, rather than the £1 bet I had intended. It's what they call a fat finger trade – instead of typing in £1 to close my trade, I've inadvertently hit the zero and put in £10. The result? My trade is closed all right. And the remaining £9 is automatically designated as a sell.

My mistake, entirely.

- I've just lost £490 on my original dud trade

- And now I have taken a huge – for me – position going the other way.

What would you have done?

1   I swear

2   I panic

3   I focus on the screen

4   The currency prices are changing all the time. In my favour. So I am able to reduce the risk on my this-is-a-mistake £9 trade by buying at £6 a point – I type the figure VERY carefully.

5   I hit the enter key to take an £18 profit

6   And I still have a £3 sell bet in place

This trade seems to be heading in the right direction. Very much so. Within three hours, prices have fallen by 100 points. At which point

I pocket £300. Which, of course, would have been £900, had I only kept my nerve and left the £9-a-point trade in play instead of correcting my mistake.

So how am I doing overall?

If it weren't for Berkeley, I'd be in profit. As it is, my trading education has cost me £1,400.

Disappointed?

Of course, but I look on this as money well spent. I'm starting to get a proper feel for the slings and arrows of outrageous fortune that may yet be coming my way.

And if my dearest friends sneer "Told You So!" I'll introduce them to Tossa the Tosa.

Chapter Sixteen

Behind the scenes in the dealing room – so near yet so far from the customer who's £750,000 in profit

Mid-July

"This spread betting thing," says Retired Reggie. "I want you to show me what it's all about."

So I take him back to my place – the first time I've taken a bloke who wasn't a washing machine mechanic back here in a long time – and sit him down in front of the computer. Then I connect to my Finspreads account.

"Welcome to the Twenty-first century," I say.

Reggie surveys the trading screen. If he notices the cash in my account is substantially less than £5000, he's too kind to say so. Instead he asks me, "How do you know these people actually exist?"

"What do you mean?"

"How do you know it's not just a couple of people in an office in Twickenham?"

"I've met the Welshman."

"An office in Cardiff, then?"

I promise Reggie I will invite myself to Finspreads Towers. Then I give him a tour of what else is available on the internet. He's still keenly interested in the rag trade, so I stick the words 'fashion design history' into Google, and there are 32 million links to choose from. We also discover that Japanese Tosas are banned in the UK. Just as well Tossa's not a pedigree.

Two days later, I travel to America Square, in the heart of the City of London. Finspreads HQ is posh. Lots of marble, mirrors and high speed lifts.

I am whooshed up to the twelfth floor, home of the dealing room. I'm hoping it's going to be like that that film *Wall Street*. The one where Michael Douglas is all red braces and bad attitude.

In my fantasy, there's a Finspreads frenzy of Masters of the Universe yelling, "SELL! SELL!" And one of them will give me some hot tips that put my account back into profit.

The reality is altogether more genteel. (In fact, I have to say I've seen more action in the stockroom of an advertising agency where I used to work.)

The first revelation is that the Welshman is clearly a lot more important than I thought. He has his own office, complete with windows and a spectacular view of Tower Bridge.

But the dealers – there are about twenty guys, mostly in their twenties – they don't get a view of anything. Presumably because if they're busy admiring Tower Bridge, they can't squint at their trading screen. Actually, each dealer has three screens on his desk.

One going up, one going down, and another going nowhere just for show… just as I am humming the chorus of *If I Was A Rich Man*, the Finspreads Head Dealer appears. He's called David Morris.

"So, tell me David," I do my best to sound as if I interview people all the time, instead of just lounging around drinking coffee, "exactly what happens when I place a trade?"

"We say here comes Sally, see what you go for, and then bet the other way," he deadpans.

This is an uncanny echo of an email I got from Brian L. He wrote: "Sally, I think you have been very brave to tell the world about your trades; I won't even tell the wife about mine! I hate to tell you this, but a well known way to make money is to follow the trades of a novice, but do the opposite. Buy when they sell. Sell when they buy."

I wrote back immediately with details of my three open buy trades – Gold, Brent Crude and the sterling/yen currency pair – and told Brian my favourite flowers are tiger lilies, but so far no florists have beaten a path to my door.

Anyway. Back on the twelfth floor. What actually happens is as follows:

Every trade placed with Finspreads – which means thousands, every day – goes into a position monitor and then gets entered into the house book.

Then the traders take a view. "Right now, everyone's buying the FTSE on recent lows," David explains. "We think that's smart, so we hedge the position in the futures market. That's how we make the money to pay out the winning trades. There will be lots of them today, because the index has climbed 30 points so far."

This is the ideal scenario, David continues. "Winning clients are happy clients, and provided we've hedged the trades, we're happy too."

What happens when the traders disagree with customer selections?

It's simple: they don't bother to hedge and if they're right and we've got it wrong, our cash goes onto their bottom line.

While I am thinking malevolently about the Berkeley Group, David continues. Most customers, apparently, are day traders. And they particularly like trading FTSE, Dow, DAX, blue chip UK stocks and currencies.

And yes, some customers are infinitely better traders than I am.

David promptly anticipates my next question – "Please may I have the names, email addresses, marital status and star signs of the most successful customers?" – and hands me over to his colleague, Angus Campbell. He's working the phones and inviting certain clients to Troon, for the golf. Clearly, these are the people I want to know more about.

So who are they?

Angus smiles an enigmatic smile. "You'll have to kill me before I tell you anything like that. But what I *can* do is this."

He fiddles with his computer keyboard, but annoyingly turns the screen so that I can't see anything, unless I sit on his lap. Since we've only just been introduced, I reluctantly decide this would be inappropriate.

"I've got a client here who's made a trading profit of £750,000, and he's currently up £30,000," Angus announces. "He trades across all markets. It's his hobby. While this gentleman…" Angus nods towards the out-of-sight screen, "We've paid him well over a million since 2001. He's amazing at picking peaks and troughs and I've known him run a loss of £20,000 in the hope it will come back. Or how about this one from Scotland – won over £250,000, trades on a daily basis, follows charts and always uses stops."

It strikes me that Angus is as I imagine an old-fashioned bank manager must once have been. He knows his customers by name but would never reveal their identities, either by seduction or torture. He talks of them fondly, almost as if they are relatives, and is genuinely pleased when they are doing well.

Angus goes on to explain that he divides Finspreads customers into two categories: winners and losers. Annoyingly, I am currently in the wrong category.

Finally on my visit I'm introduced to the Customer Services Department. These are the people you talk to when you want to convert your electronic winnings back into real, spendable moolah. A joyful moment that I have yet to experience. I spend five minutes gossiping with Maria. She is renowned for being exceptionally cheerful when customers call. Little do they realise that this is because her screensaver features George Clooney and Brad Pitt.

"Are they clients, too?" I ask?

Maria blushes. "No comment."

Chapter Seventeen
September

Trader's block and a four-legged Dow Jones

I am suffering from trader's block.

After eight – EIGHT – consecutive losers, costing me a total of £429, I have lost the will to trade. You name it, and I've been losing on it.

Remember there was talk of an Abbey National takeover? I followed the money just as the wise were pocketing their profits.

Then I heard Reuters was the worst performing share in the FTSE 100. I now hold myself directly responsible for its subsequent recovery.

As for the rest, all I will say – in retrospect – is that it is not prudent to place trades merely to take your mind off the fact that your 74-year-old Uncle David has inadvertently flooded your bathroom while in the process of fitting a new kitchen.

Amidst this chaos, I am receiving more and more emails from Finspreads customers. My Berkeley catastrophe seems to have struck a chord. Suddenly everyone is writing to me with their own hard luck stories. I have become an Agony Aunt, without ever applying for the job.

Feeling wholly unqualified, I nonetheless respond diligently to all my correspondents – a great excuse for not writing my novel – while licking my own wounds.

Frankly, one or two of these messages are a little alarming. Especially the ones that begin, "Dearest Sally, my wife doesn't understand me, but I know that you do." Whenever anyone says they're worried by their losses, I always remind them of my dad's Golden Rule – never gamble more than you can afford to throw into the gutter. Not only is this essential, but also I don't want to get caught up in some tabloid sting. Imagine the headlines: Spread Betting Agony Aunt Loser Encourages Others Into Debt.

After the rubbish trades, my total losses to date are £1,500. In fact, my ego is taking a bigger battering than my bank balance. I keep getting it wrong. I am accustomed to getting it correct in other areas of my life (excluding romance). So how come this spread betting business is so difficult?

"Treat it as though it's a business," comes one sensible email. "Accept that there's a learning curve, and that your losses are the equivalent of start-up costs."

That makes me feel better. As does this message from Pat, who lives in Cornwall and comments: "Quickly trundling through what you've written so far, I see you have trodden a well-travelled path, me included. 'Oh dear.' I expect you are saying to yourself. 'What do I have to do to make profits?' A crossroads indeed. The foolish carry on and throw more money at it and lose that as well. The wise seek help from someone who knows and paper trades meantime or quit."

I am no quitter. And it's too soon to go to paper (hypothetical) trading. But I have had to accept that my short – very short – run of beginner's luck has evidently run its path, and that I am in danger of becoming trapped in a downward spiral.

So what do I do next?

Well, having picked so many dogs myself, I've decided to buy a real one. He is a Parson Jack Russell. Eleven weeks old, and absolutely gorgeous. Good enough to eat – Tossa's already tried to take a bite out of him, but he bravely stood his ground.

I have named him Dow Jones.

Dow-Wow, for short.

Chapter Eighteen

Expert advice takes me in a new direction

One Week Later

"What you need to do," says the email from a well-wisher called Tony, "is invest five hundred quid in Sandy Jadeja's one day course. The problem is, it will not make good copy, nor will it seem to be anything other than a free plug for his services. However, if you want to make money out of trading, it could well make sense."

Sandy Jadeja doesn't have to be expensive. In fact, he regularly gives free seminars to Finspreads clients. And even if he turns out to be as dull as Albania on a wet Wednesday, I certainly need some help.

When I began writing, I envisaged a few little scrapes along the way. But by the time we got this far, I was planning to be in the driving seat of something other than a runaway train on a steep, downhill gradient.

I contact the Welshman to ask if Sandy might be able to help. Even before I can say, "I'm willing to pay," he tells me he thinks it's a great idea.

Will the Guru of Finspreads be able to help me? While I'm waiting for an answer, I swap a few more emails with Tony.

Tony explains why going on Sandy's course will fail to entertain my readers. "People think trading is exciting and fast-moving," he says. "One moment you're ten thousand up, then you're twenty thousand down. One minute you're in gold, then you're in brent crude. Then you're short the FTSE. They think it's a white knuckle ride, all thrills and spills. But Sandy – he teaches a cool, calm system. No drama, no thrills, no nasty surprises. You target something to happen. If it does, you open your trade, set very tight stop levels, work out where to exit the trade with a profit, put in your limit order and forget about it."

Call me a wuss, but cool and calm sounds much more fun than watching my £5,000 starter bank dribbling away.

However, there's a problem.

Sandy phones to tell me I can't come on his course. "You don't know enough, yet," he explains. "You'd be out of your depth. Waste of time and money. And what's that terrible noise in the background?"

Dow Jones has his paws on the windowsill. He's barking at Tossa – already the size of a four-year-old – who is dragging Much Divorced Michael along the street. I lob today's copy of the FT at my dog, so I can hear Sandy speak.

"I've decided to give you a private coaching session." Sandy's tone of voice suggests he's a man who relishes a challenge.

So yesterday, we sat down together. Sandy doesn't pull any punches, which is just as well, because Dow-Wow is balanced precariously on his knee.

Sandy starts, "It's said that you trade your personality. So far as I can tell, you're a schizophrenic." He edges his chair slightly away from mine. This diagnosis turns out not to be as bad as it sounds. Sandy has identified that I've been dabbling. A little bit of this. A little bit of that. Or as I prefer to call it, experimenting.

"So what's your trading plan?" he demands.

"Er, well."

Er–well, indeed.

Thirty minutes later, and I am the proud possessor of a Trading Plan. It's pinned to the notice board in my office, so that Dow-Wow can't get his needle-sharp teeth into it.

My Plan is as follows:

1 Conserve remaining funds.

2 Refrain from entering reckless trades for no good reason.

3 Rely much more on charts.

4 Rely much less on gut feeling.

5 Avoid heavy losses: not only will I fix stop-losses, but I'll actually stick to them, instead of cancelling them when my limit is about to be breached because I'm still hopeful the trade will return to profit. It rarely gets better – I just end up losing even more.

6   My immediate objective is to understand what I am doing, and restore my confidence with some winning trades.

7   My longer-term objective is to get back to break-even, before moving into profit.

"So what are you going to trade?" Sandy asks.

By now, I've got the hang of his technique: like all good coaches, Sandy doesn't tell you what to do. Instead, he makes you do the work.

"I've been following sterling and the yen." Does this make me sound like a stalker?

"Too volatile for someone in your position. You'll lose too much too fast if you get it wrong."

Don't I know it. "How about the Dow Jones?"

Recognising his name, Dow-Wow stirs in his sleep.

I favour the Dow, because the markets in America don't start trading until 2.30pm our time. Which means they wake up about the same time I do. And besides, I've named my dog in honour of the index. So my choice is entirely rational.

It meets Sandy's approval, too. He reckons I should stick to trading one particular market from now on, instead of playing the field and spreading myself too thin.

We move on to discuss my preferred trading period. Am I a day trader? A longer-term position trader? Or somewhere in-between?

I think I'm in-between. I don't want to have to watch the screen all the time, and would be happy to hold my position for a few days or more. Especially if it's winning.

Next, Sandy produces a series of charts. He decides to explain them in terms that match my alleged occupation. "The market is a language," he tells me. "It tells a story. In essence, it is a mystery that unfolds before your eyes, minute by minute, hour by hour, day by day. Every day, in every market, four things happen. The market opens. It closes. It records a high. And it records a low. That's its structure. It really is that simple." Sandy allows himself a smile before adding, "And it really is that complicated, in that no-one on earth can be certain what's going to happen."

So back to the Dow. For the past few weeks it's been rising. And, as of now, I shall be following that trend. Thanks to Sandy, I now understand when to place a trade (basically, once I'm reasonably sure the Dow will continue to go up!) and where to set my stop-losses.

I have promised to look at the charts instead of relying on impulse and wishful thinking laced with optimism. I know how much I'm prepared to lose as a result of consulting recent lows – if the Dow falls below these, then I'm out.

How can I possibly go wrong?

Chapter Nineteen

What happens when I ignore expert advice?

Late October

Reports of my death have been greatly exaggerated, although not entirely.

First of all, I am suffering from a bruised heart.

Filthy Lucca.

Again.

He turned up out of the blue three weeks ago – all glossy hair and six pack – determined to give me another taste of *la dolce vita*. I closed my eyes to such obvious questions as, 'Where have you been for the last eighteen months, four weeks and three days?" and allowed him to romance me. This time, I even introduced him to Retired Reggie and Much Divorced Michael. I could tell they didn't really like him.

Tossa had the right idea. She peed copiously over his Gucci loafers.

Despite this minor hiccup, we shared five magical days together before he mentioned he's getting married after Christmas. But not to me…

After which, I became so accustomed to blowing my nose, that it took me a couple of days to realise despair had matured into flu. I retired to my bed with only Dow-Wow and *The Daily Mail* for company. Curiously enough, the Mail gave me the will to live and trade again.

The newspaper is waging war on the Government's proposed new Gambling Bill. There's page after page of dire warnings about the Evils of Gambling – enough to make me want to offer odds on which raindrop will get to the bottom of the window first.

How come the Government is encouraging us to gamble, while telling us we can no longer smoke – except, perhaps, in Supercasinos – or hunt foxes?

There is only one thing to do. I dose myself with Lemsip, shuffle into the office, and log on to Finspreads.

I checked out my recent trades, to remind myself what had happened after my lesson from Sandy Jadeja – I'd tried to practise what he'd preached. But the Dow had failed to co-operate, resulting in another eight consecutive losing trades. At least now I had got into the stop-loss habit – and my total losses amounted to only £175.27.

"Bravo!" I hear you chortle.

I did not share that opinion: it felt like death by a thousand cuts. Then, as I say, Filthy Lucca turned up and spread betting was the last thing on my mind.

But now...

I need something to take my mind off my disastrous love life. I scowl at the Dow, and then consult Yahoo to see which shares are doing well.

One name stands out a mile.

Google.

A site I adore and use dozens of times every day, although that's beside the point (I think).

Google went public back in the summer, and from the day the company made its stock market debut, the share price has been all one-way: it just keeps rocketing up.

My days of being a smart-arse and thinking, "In that case, it's definitely going to reverse," are over. I'm going with the trend.

A nagging little voice reminds me about Sandy's good advice: that I should steer well clear of volatile markets, on the grounds that I will lose too much too fast when I get it wrong.

I know what Sandy will say if I consult him about Google. One look at the chart shows me the company's share price can easily move three or four dollars in a day. In spread betting terms, where every cent equals one point, that makes Google volatile – spelt s-t-e-e-r c-l-e-a-r.

Thinking I can always plead that the balance of my mind has been affected by my Benylin cough medicine – the label warns you not to operate machinery when you swig it, and I guess that includes computers – I place a buy trade for 50p a point.

Five minutes later, while I am still pondering exactly where to place my stop-loss, I am down £65. Google, it seems, can in fact go down as suddenly, quickly and easily as any Premiership striker in the opposition penalty box.

My finger hovers over the SELL button. I shall cut my losses, go back to bed and prepare to die, choking on a Fisherman's Friend. And then the miracle happens: a coughing fit so bad I have to walk away from the computer, in search of water.

By the time I return, I am only losing £15.

What would YOU have done? Taken the loss?

Neither did I.

I sit tight. Fortune favours the brave, or so they say (except, I suspect, in Iraq).

By the end of the session, I have banked £200. Over the next few days, as I grow sicker and sicker, I win more and more. Three separate, consecutive winning trades: £100, £319 and £436.45.

There's currently £4,233.63 in my Finspreads account and getting back to break-even of £5,000 is looking eminently possible.

Chapter Twenty

Why I decide to dump my biggest winner

1st January 2005

After my spectacular success on Google, I was reluctant to enter the market again.

If Filthy Lucca had taught me anything – apart from the fact that I'm even worse at picking men than I am at picking trades – it was that dangerous liaisons always end in tears.

And Google had been so perfect...

There was only one thing to do. I walked away.

Our relationship had been more than a one-night stand, but it clearly wasn't going to go the distance. If ever there was a time to quit while I was ahead, this was it.

And yet I was now Miss Google. I'd received a ton of email from people wanting to know if they should buy all the Google they could afford, and then sit on their trades.

"ABSOLUTELY NOT!" I typed. I didn't want the responsibility of anyone else following my example. I also pointed out that my biggest win – £436.45 – was the result of a 50p stake, which meant Google had shifted 872 points. They don't come more volatile than that.

And what goes up must eventually come down. For example:

- On 15 November 2004, Google closed at $184.87

- Five sessions later, the price touched $161.31

- In which case, a 50p buy trade would have resulted in a loss of 2356 points – or £1,178

While my dearest friends signed their Christmas cards, I continued to monitor the Google share price. It was almost as bad as being in love. I'd grin from ear to ear every time I thought about Google. Bore the latterati with my tales of Google. Dream of Google. Believe me, I was even thinking of sending Christmas cards to Larry Page and Sergey Brin.

But in my heart I already knew the truth. If Google was a car, it was a Ferrari. While I was a driver with a provisional licence. And even though the trend was onwards and upwards, there were still enough short-term reversals to make me skid.

"Adieu, Google." I deleted the name from my Finspreads screen. "It's been great, and I'll treasure the memory. But we both know that if we carry on meeting like this we'll spoil what we had. Much as I love you, I simply can't afford you any more."

And that was how I came to quit while I was ahead.

Christmas came and went. The biggest surprise being that Retired Reggie has joined the computer set. A gift from his nephew. He's excited and terrified that he's going to make a twat of himself.

"Are you going to use it to do that spread betting thing?" I asked.

"Actually, I thought I might do a spot of research into my family tree." Reggie's parents came originally from Poland.

Much Divorced Michael, meanwhile, received a decree nisi for Christmas. He still doesn't understand why Wife Number Five – Holly, wasn't it? – terminated him with such prejudice.

Last night at midnight, we stood on the top of Primrose Hill, toasted one another with champagne and watched the fireworks explode over the River Thames.

I wonder what the New Year will bring?

Chapter Twenty-one

There's a market worth $1.5 trillion a day I'll have some of that!

March

Every once in a while I get an email from a Finspreads customer that asks what my novel's about.

It's a thriller. Set just slightly in the future. It features members of the Royal Family, although it's not about them. The hero is Jack Hollander, an American student, who discovers a secret that, if it's true, could finish off the monarchy for good. And the dramatic centre of the story: will Jack get to the truth before a bunch of villains who make up The Sceptre Committee – a *very* secret society – get to him? If you like a good conspiracy, you'll love my book.

I'm meant to be writing this story full-time. Indeed, I have been leading the life of a writer in all respects – apart from the actual writing bit. Instead, I have been behaving as though I have a large private income. That's OK for Much Divorced Michael, whose grandfather invented some plastic lid or other and made a zillion. Lately, my conscience has been pricking me – not least because my mum and my brother keep asking me how the novel is coming along.

"Slowly," is the best that I can manage.

As for the spread betting. My New Year Resolution had been to get back to break-even and then quit. (Just like Nick Leeson.) I've been wondering what's the fastest way to make the £766.38 I need to declare a profit.

I'm telling myself I'm too busy to trade. But I think I'm fooling myself. The reality is that I have moved from Greed to Fear. Having revelled in a winning streak, I don't want to lose again..

A phone call.

The Welshman invites me to lunch.

"I'm not sure what to trade," I confess. We're sharing a plate of barbecued smoked octopus that tastes nicer than you might imagine.

"Well, your trading style to date is rather like this meal." He gestures at our tapas selection. "Most of our successful traders don't do that."

This is interesting. The Welshman's finally going to spill the (figurative) beans. I lean forward.

"Think about becoming a specialist. Just trade one or two markets, instead of spreading yourself too thin."

More or less the same advice I'd received from Sandy Jadeja. It makes sense, but *which* markets should I trade? The Welshman's not saying.

I return home to discover Dow Jones sorting my post. Helpfully, he has gnawed his way through most of today's arrivals:

- A bank statement that reveals my savings are holding out.

- A local newspaper that tells me Camden plans to increase parking charges. Again.

- A honeymoon postcard from Filthy Lucca. "Weather is lovely. Wish you were here." I hand this to Dow-Wow and encourage him to chew.

- A flyer advertising a new local Italian restaurant.

- A padded envelope that turns out to be gift from John Bartlett. He of the spread betting for beginners course I attended last year.

John has sent me a DVD called Currency Trading For Beginners. No time like the present. I load it up, and off we go.

The market for forex – that's the professionals' abbreviation for foreign exchange – is worth $1.5 trillion a day, I learn. Sounds promising. Surely I can pick up a few points along the way. I listen intently to the DVD soundtrack. "Which way is the market moving? How far up will it go? And when will it go the other way?"

Alas, there are no ready answers to these pertinent questions. I go through the chapters from start to finish. It's almost a refresher course in spread betting basics, as applied to currencies. I'm foolish enough to ignore the section that wants me to download trading software; it seems like too great a commitment.

Nonetheless, I am encouraged to try a spot of currency trading, and I cast my eye over sterling against the dollar. I'd been visiting an old friend in New York the previous month (where, incidentally, guns are legal but spread betting is not) and I had gleefully taken full advantage of sterling's buying power. There's a clear trend, and I decide to follow it.

My first attempt to buy ends in failure. The sterling/dollar Daily Cash – the market with the narrowest spread, best for day trading – spat out my 50p trade, informing me the minimum trade is £2 a point. Too scary. I retreat, and sit watching my chart. I'll trade the March futures contract instead; the spread's wider but I can stick to the minimum 50p stake.

At the risk of sounding smug, I time it beautifully. The minute-by-minute chart is going up and down like an Alpine range. Instead of feeling I need to trade right away, at all costs, I've learned instead to be patient. I wait until the price has just lurched down in a big, satisfying spike, then buy at $1.9061. Immediately, the price began to rise. It's great when this happens, especially as most of the time when I place a trade, the opposite occurs – in the past I've felt as though I personally can move markets. The wrong way.

A couple of hours later and I'm 67 points up.

- I adjust my stop-loss to lock in some profit, and ensure the worst that can happen is that I'll end up with a tenner. (FEAR)

- But then again, why take the risk? I sell the trade for a profit of £33.50. (GREED)

- Next time I check, the price is still rising. (PISSED OFF)

I place a new buy trade.

The price has risen to $1.9199.

Chapter Twenty-two

A series of unfortunate events

April

Maybe I should confine my foreign exchange trading activities to occasional visits to Heathrow Airport's Bureau de Change.

April has been the cruellest month.

After my initial forex win, I was proceeding with optimistic caution. In other words, I fixed my stop-losses the moment I made my trades. This swiftly resulted in two successive losing trades for a net deficit of £63.

You can probably guess what happened next. I had a knee-jerk reaction and vowed, "Never mind, I'll get it all back. Now."

My next mistake was to decide the quickest way to retrieve my money would be to increase my stake. That way, I didn't need the market to move so much, in order to win.

Finally, I compounded my folly by believing – on the basis of nothing much more than a gut instinct – that the falling market would continue to fall.

In less time than it took me to write that last paragraph, I placed a £2 sell trade on the March futures at $1.9138.

Retribution was swift.

By the time I had figured out where to stick my stop-loss, the dollar was perking up – simply out of malice, so far as I could tell – and I was losing £58.

"OK," I said to myself, "remember the same thing happened with Google, and that turned out all right. Simply divide by four. If you'd placed the usual 50p trade, you'd only be losing £14.50. You can live with that."

Having made my decision, I watched in rabbit-in-the-headlights fascination as my losses continued to accumulate. In the space of just eight minutes, the dollar recouped every point it had lost in the previous seventy-two hours. And then a few more.

I pulled the plug when I was losing £152, having discovered the recovery was due to Federal Reserve Chairman Alan Greenspan – he's America's equivalent to the Governor of the Bank of England – suggesting that a national sales tax would fuel economic growth. Just to make my happiness complete, by the time I'd mustered sufficient enthusiasm to revisit Finspreads the following Monday, the market was back below $1.9138. In other words, if I'd kept my nerve for a few more days, I'd have lost nothing at all.

You have to be in it to win it, as they say. So the next day, back I went with a £1 buy bet on the June contract. This time, I got it right, and banked £50.

Which I proceeded to return the day after.

"At least I'm beginning to get a feel for this market", I told myself. "The trend is clearly up." I duly bought £1 of the June £/$ with increased confidence: it seemed to me that there was scope to make 100 points, before collecting my winnings.

Yeah, right.

I'd better type what happened next with my eyes closed, because I still can't bear to think about it. It's a bit like Lemony Snicket's Series of Unfortunate Events:

1   For a few days, my trade doesn't seem to be going anywhere. A bit into profit, but not worth taking. Then a small loss, but nothing to fret about.

2   A week passes. My trade is down £33. This feels like a buying opportunity. I place a second £1 trade. When I check out prices an hour later, the two trades show a combined profit of £8.

3   Another five days pass. I'm now in a spot of bother. If you really must know, I'm losing £559. (Guess who didn't put an immediate stop-loss on when placing the trades and then didn't bother to check the market when it fell 250 points between Friday night and Monday afternoon?) Then again, it's only lost money if I close the trade. I'll wait for the market to overcome its temporary blip and recover.

4   The following morning, the market seems to be going my way. I place a new £2 trade. I intend to take a quick profit, so I choose the sterling/dollar Daily Cash, as it has the narrowest spread.

5   At 3.26 that afternoon, US interest rates rise by 0.25%. The impact is immediate: I lose £328 while asking Dow-Wow, "WHYYYYYYYYYY?" It feels like falling from a plane and being so interested in the way the earth is moving that you forget to pull the rip cord. My trade expires at the end of the day, so I'm saddled with my losses.

6   They say repeating the same action and expecting a different result is a formula for madness. The following day, I again buy into the daily market. Again, the market disagrees, and again I am strangely reluctant to bale out.

7   This time, though, I don't quite crash and burn. I manage to pluck just a little sliver of triumph from disaster. I switch horses in mid-stream. First, I close my trade, accepting a loss of £202. Then I switch from buying to selling. The market continues to fall and I eventually claw back £116.

My sterling/dollar initiatives had resulted in a net loss of £641. That, alas, is not the end of The Tale of Woe.

I still have two trades on the June sterling/dollar in play. And they continue to go the wrong way. At one point I was £1,043 down. My current strategy is somewhere between denial, allied to a genuine belief – based on the charts – that some time between now and June, the dollar will weaken again. After all, America's payroll figures were good last week, and that reduced my nominal losses to a mere £531.

Not great, but at least by keeping the trade open, I'd avoided having £1,043 debited from my account.

Today, while catching up with my Diary, I've been keeping a closer-than-usual eye on the market. It's been rising steadily since last Thursday, and there was a sudden steep climb to a new April high at about lunchtime.

I've learned that a rapid climb usually means an equally rapid retreat, and with this in mind, I sold £2 of the Daily Spot.

Guess what happened next?

Ha! This time, you're wrong!

In less than an hour, I made a profit of £112. I wish I could sit here and tell you I was aware that the American trade deficit figures were due. And that they soared to an all-time high of £61.04 billion in February.

Frankly, I was just lucky.

Unlike Much Divorced Michael.

Who are these people who reported us to Camden's Environmental Health Department, just because Tossa was trying to help by cleaning their plates with his tongue? The poor dog's been threatened with an ASBO.

From now on, the latterati will be obliged to meet across the road, at Primrose Hill's newest restaurant.

Chapter Twenty-three

Making money from the Government

May

Retired Reggie is having a stroke. His face is contorted and he's hissing unintelligible words at me through the side of his mouth.

"Gon't gook lound. Gaul Gigarney. Hind ooo."

Much Divorced Michael is swifter on the uptake. "You're kidding!" He swivels his head. "Blimey. It is him!"

We're doing coffee in our new hang-out, J's. I follow Michael's open-mouthed gaze. Nothing prepares you for the shock of coming face to face with a living legend, eating his breakfast.

You get every variety of celebrity passing through Primrose Hill. But this is AAA List: Sir Paul McCartney is munching away on the Vegetarian Breakfast Special.

We fall silent, almost as though we are in church. Unlike my companions, I'm too young to remember when the release of a new

Beatles record was a cause for national celebration. But I know all the songs, because my Big Brother used to sing them around the house. And out of all the Beatles, Paul was always my favourite. I guess I have a bit of a thing for older men.

Paul's little daughter is wearing a bib that says 'I Love My Dad'. She's bored with breakfast, and she toddles right towards us. In fact, right towards ME. She's spotted Dow Jones, and he's spotted her.

And now Paul has spotted his baby spotting my dog. He springs to his feet to supervise proceedings.

Fortunately, Tossa is across the road at the pet shop, having a bath. Dow-Wow is much better with kids. He just stands there looking adorable. As does Paul, who leans down and starts scratching Dow Jones behind the ears; the sign of a man who knows his dogs.

Having broken the ice, we all spend the next fifteen minutes talking about dogs and kids. We pretend not to recognise Paul McCartney. He pretends not to be Paul McCartney, although the Scouse accent remains surprisingly strong.

After he's gone, we debate whether we should shave Dow-Wow and sell his fur on eBay.

"Are you short of a few bob, Sally?" asks Reggie. I wonder uncomfortably if he's become sufficiently computer literate to be able to go onto the Finspreads web site and read my blog.

"Actually, I made a few bob on the election," I retort.

Even though we had just endured the most boring election campaign EVER, and we all knew the outcome would be as predictable as any ballot in Stalin's Russia or Bush's America, there had at least been the consolation of making a few bob with Finspreads.

Unlike trading, or the inner workings of the City, politics is something I actually understand. Ever since I was a badly-behaved kid, and my parents threatened that unless I mended my ways Margaret Thatcher would come and sort me out, I've been interested in the psychology of politics.

For instance, the moment John Major whipped out his soapbox, in Cheltenham Spa of all places, I knew the Tories would come from behind and contrary to all expectations deny Neil Kinnock the keys to No 10. An inspired piece of electioneering. But because this was back in the dark age of 1992, long before Finspreads was a twinkle in anybody's eyes, I'd been obliged to dent the profits of William Hill, by making a series of bets on the size of the Conservative majority. I spent my winnings on a holiday in Spain.

Five years later, when Tony Blair swept into Downing Street on the back of his landslide victory, I was once again on the winning side. I even voted for the man; he looked like a pretty straight kind of guy to me. He won again next time Britain went to the ballot box – and so did I.

Which brings us to 4th May 2005.

This time, two big questions.

1   Who should I vote for? My dilemma was complicated by the absence of a Monster Loony candidate in Holborn & St Pancras.

2   What should I do about my disastrous Buy bets on the June sterling/dollar? With time marching towards the expiry date, I

seemed to be not so much in-for-a-penny-in-for-a-pound as down about five hundred quid.

Someone would have to pay. I thought it might as well be Tony Blair.

But first, I consulted the Welshman. "Who's in charge of making the market for the election specials?" I enquired. "I'd like to ask a few questions." Get a few tips, more like it.

"Leave it to me," he said.

Imagine my surprise when, an hour later, I received an email from ACampbell@finspreads.com. I kid you not. That really was the address. Was this a case of Spinspreads? And if so, did they know more than I knew? Then I remembered. Not the Downing Street Machiavelli, but the guy who'd been inviting high roller Finspreads customers to the golf.

We exchanged electronic banter.

"Are novelty bets like this popular?" I asked.

"Clients love these markets, and we've taken quite a lot of business," Mr Campbell responded.

"And how's the market trending?"

"Lots of Labour majority buying. Our price started at a majority of 50 – 55. It's been going up ever since."

"Do you think the customers have got it right?"

"These markets are probably the best poll there is out there. It's opinion, backed by money."

I waited until the eve of polling day before taking time out from filling in my stack of postal votes (don't worry, that's a joke) to place my trades.

No matter what the opinion polls asserted, my gut was telling me Labour's massive majority was in for a good kicking. Dozens of Blairites were about to get their P45s, and serve them right. Not only because of the war, but because of what New Labour has done to education-education-education, all the phoney jobs they've created in the public sector (if all else fails, perhaps I shall become a £25,000 p.a. five-a-day fruit and veg adviser) and Tony Blair's justification for identity cards: "They will be useful if you want to rent a video." Yep, he really did say that.

And, yes, I know we are advised against trading when we feel emotional. Nevertheless. I gleefully sold a Labour majority of 87. They couldn't possibly do that well. And once I'd placed this first trade, simple mathematics dictated the rest:

- Conservative seats: BUY @ 191

- Labour seats: SELL @ 364

- Lib Dem seats: SELL @ 67

Which brings us to election night itself.

Moments after the polls closed, the BBC was predicting a Labour win with a majority of 66 seats. I settled down to enjoy the show. My favourite moment was the result from the Cardiff North, where a woman from the Vote Dream Party set a new record for the fewest votes received at an election. She received precisely one vote, and it subsequently emerged that she couldn't have voted for herself, since she was registered in a different constituency.

On to the morning after the night before. How much had I won? Finspreads wasn't going to tell me until the last vote was counted.

While I was waiting for the polling officials in Northern Ireland and the Shetlands to get their acts together, I found myself obliged to think about my two outstanding currency bets. They'd been lingering like a rotting cabbage, and at one point I'd been over £1,000 down, although lately the exchange rate was swinging back in my favour.

Now comes the tragic bit.

About two weeks ago, I was almost into profit. One trade was £4 up, and the other only £29 down. I felt wonderful. Vindicated. My long wait was about to pay off. Profit beckoned. Thank goodness I'd kept my nerve and refused to accept a four-figure loss.

The following day I was losing £51.

So I waited.

And waited.

Right this moment, I'm losing £723.

Next time it gets to break-even I'm getting out, I promise.

Meanwhile, I've just won a total of 36 points from my election bets, which translated into a modest £80.

Why on earth was I so timid?

Chapter Twenty-four

Is this the darkest hour?

June

I was due to visit my mother. She'd been making lots of maternal noises, wanting to know how my novel was going and asking, "When will you be going back to work, dear?"

Novel writing's not work? I avoided her question, but there was no getting away from the guilt. I duly returned to my neglected thriller.

A successful session. The plot is thickening nicely, although I'm getting far too fond of one of the villains – Barry Bell, the sixty-third richest man in England – and I'm still nowhere near finished.

But still. Every word takes me closer to the end.

Until…

One moment I'm pounding my laptop keyboard. The next, the letter O has sheared off and I'm holding it in my hand. It is, to say the least, inconvenient: My hero's surname is Hollander.

I – briefly – consider changing it. But Jack Dutch or even Jack Hullander just doesn't have the right ring to it.

Fortunately, there's an obvious solution: Superglue.

OK, if you learn one thing from my experiences, it's this: never use superglue to repair your computer keyboard. Never. Ever.

After I have finished sobbing, I call the computer guy. He performs open heart surgery on my machine. It doesn't come cheap. But at least my Story of O has a happy ending.

Which brings me to those two currency trades. They were still in play at the end of last week when I departed to visit my mum. Still losing me money... I decided to let sterling fight back against the dollar while I was away.

Bad things about the visit:

- My mum thinks I should go back into advertising.

- My mum thinks I should find a nice man and get married.

- My mum doesn't rate Dow Jones as a surrogate grandson.

My mum can't stop banging on about how well my Big Brother is doing: his job blah blah, his lovely wife blah blah, their gorgeous kids blah blah.

- Good things about the visit:

- My mum takes me shopping to Bicester Village.

- I emerge triumphant with a sequined handbag.

- Plus three pairs of shoes.

- And a drop-dead gorgeous black dress.

But it turns out I've been shopping while Rome is burning. The sterling/dollar exchange rate is approaching its 52-week low. Nothing to worry about if you happen to be on holiday in America – just a little less spending power. Back in North London, however, I am now down a grand total of £1,700. And to think, a couple of weeks earlier I could have closed both trades for a loss of only £25.

Should I return the handbag? Tell the shop assistants of Bicester my black dress is the wrong colour and demand my money back? I endure a bad night's sleep.

The next day, I realise I am now locked deep into the Ostrich Position: head in the sand, not wanting to know, and starting to experience something very like morning sickness whenever I check the status of my trades.

I have only one card left to play. I decide to run away. I go back online and book a rail ticket to Penzance – the train to John O'Groats has already left. I pack a suitcase, and while I'm waiting for the cab to Paddington, I hedge my bets. Sort of. Finally, I place a stop-loss on one trade to capitulate if it reaches a loss of £1,000. If only I'd done that at the beginning! I leave the other trade to fend for itself.

In Cornwall, I contemplate my failure as a trader, my failure as a writer, my inability to find a decent bloke and the fact that I have forgotten to renew my library books. Apart from that, it's just the break I need.

Back home a few days later, I discover my stop-loss has been activated on the first trade – I have lost £1,000 – and the clock is ticking on the other. For the next few days, when I check my account status, I feel as though I am visiting a hospice. I pay my respects once a day, and am thankful when the visit is over.

I remember what Sandy Jadeja said about how we trade our personality. And realise I am a hopeless, hopeless optimist. My dearest friends assure me this is because I have failed to understand the plot where life is concerned. But I can't help it. I believe in happy endings:

- I am certain my novel will get finished, published and become a best seller – even in the face of overwhelming evidence to the contrary.

- Tottenham Hotspur will win the Premiership. Eventually.

- Somewhere, there's another man who's just waiting to break my heart.

- I still think I can crack spread betting. Even though the second trade has expired for a loss of £893. Which leaves my Finspreads balance at £1,478.13.

"We told you this spread betting business would never work out." My dearest friends try hard to keep a triumphant edge from their words. And fail.

Chapter Twenty-five

I give up spread betting and make a new friend

A Few Days Later

Tossa has celebrated her first birthday. She is no beauty, but compensates by being fearless, brave and bold. That's a polite way of saying she is an insurance claim waiting to happen.

While I was in Cornwall, Tossa stole a sandwich from the mouth of a four-year-old who was picnicking in the park. The following day, she went one better and picked a fight with a St Bernard. Much Divorced Michael has agreed to enrol his pet and himself into dog training classes.

By way of apology, he's invited the owner of the St Bernard to meet us all for a coffee at J's. By the time I arrive, Reggie has already made his big announcement. Having gained his European Computer Driving Licence – which is more than I have – and become an accomplished silver surfer, Reggie's coming out of retirement! He's discovered international employment bulletin boards and clicked his way to a design consultancy job with some company in Prague.

"What will you be doing?" I enquire.

"Stealing designs from Marks and Spencer and Topshop and modifying them for the Central European market," he grins.

If I were still spread betting, I'd short their shares.

The conversation drifts, and the St Bernard owner is talking about the intricacies of looking after three daughters, all under the age of five. "It's the hardest thing I've ever done," says Supermum.

What did you do before you had them?" I'm being polite. She looks like a nice woman, and it's decent of her not to have reported Michael for having an out-of-control dog.

"Oh, I used to be a trader. Hedge funds. That sort of thing." Supermum's eyes tell me she is connecting with her previous life. "One thing though," she sighs. "Trading used to come to an end. Looking after kids doesn't."

I make a sympathetic face. "So this trading business. Were you any good at it?"

"Er, yes."

"Let me buy you another Café Mocca." I volunteer. "Extra chocolate?"

Chapter Twenty-six

The Welshman's final words of encouragement help me back to winning ways

July

I get a call from the Welshman.

He invites me to lunch, but it feels more like a summons. I make my way to the restaurant wondering if I should resign my position as the Finspreads Blogger and Agony Aunt before I am fired.

Given my dismal trading record, it is no less than I deserve. I'm definitely not the Finspreads poster girl. They might as well have a link to my adventures that reads 'Abandon Hope All Ye Who Click Here'.

The news turns out to be even worse.

I fear the Welshman himself has been sacked. And it is probably all my fault. "Changes within the Group... I've been reassigned... Looking forward to the new challenge," he mumbles. I feel well enough for dessert only when he reassures me he still has his office with the splendid view of Tower Bridge.

I offer my resignation.

"Why would you want to do that?" The Welshman's surprise seems genuine.

"Have you *read* my stuff lately?"

"Of course. What's the problem?" The Welshman brushes aside my protests and reassures me that according to the market research, I am well popular.

As we go our separate ways, I come to the conclusion that Finspreads are pretty brave, letting someone like me tell it how it's been. Are my experiences typical? I get plenty of email from winning traders. Some just boast, but others go out of their way to help a newcomer. It's not their fault I'm so crap. Judging from my email, there are plenty of Finspreads winners. Just a shame I'm not one of them.

Oh, and did I really hear the Welshman whisper: "Decide what you think will, for certain, happen. Then trade precisely the opposite way." I ponder his advice as I would a fortune cookie, all the way home.

Two days later.

7th July 2005.

An email from Sean O'C arrives. The subject line reads Moral Dilemma. "Enjoy reading your experiences," it goes. "Here is one from me and, I'm sure, others on this awful day. I knew the FTSE100 was a good short this morning. Once news of the terrorist attacks across London was confirmed the FTSE tanked. I was suddenly faced with this moral dilemma of making money from a very bad thing or pulling out. I pulled out and watched the FTSE disappear into the abyss. I was OK about it at first, but now feel badly shaken by the experience. Upset by the terrible events. And angry at myself for not being ruthless. I am new to spread betting and the amounts in question are small, but significant in terms of confidence. What would you have done?"

It's a question of what I've already done.

Like most of us, I first checked that my loved ones were safe and well. Then I found myself compulsively riveted to the news. Lots of discussion about how the markets would respond to the outrage, and how long it would take for them to recover.

Remembering the Welshman's final remark, I promptly placed a £1 buy bet, shortly before the opening bell on the NYSE, with the DOW languishing in the pre-market at 10,143 – about 130 points down.

Minute by minute, the market has been recovering.

But now, having read S's email, I feel morally reprehensible. Upset that I am profiting from such a vile situation.

I call Supermum, former ace trader and my new mentor, to see if she thinks I'm wicked.

The answer comes without hesitation. "I lost friends at Cantor Fitzgerald on 9/11," she tells me, "so it's something we've all spent hours thinking about and discussing. But remember, the terrorists' prime aim is destabilisation. They'd love to wreck the Western economy. So if traders and other investors support the market by refusing to sell, and buying in the aftermath of an attack, it's a good thing. Much, much better than the market going into freefall and taking months to recover."

The next day, I close my July Dow futures trade for a profit of £200. And feel good about it.

Then comes another email.

"I have been spread betting small amounts for about two years," writes Andrew H. This summer started really well. I had nine consecutive winning trades, and a profit of £1,800 in one month. The problem was that after a few wins in a row, I needed to win every trade. It didn't matter if I won only £1, so long as I won. I think I got my inspiration from Arsenal a couple of years ago.

"Like you, I fancied the sterling/dollar exchange rate. It had fallen from $1.92 to $1.84, so I thought it was bound to rise. And anyway, I was invincible! So I bet £1 to rise, with no stop-loss.

"It fell.

"I bet another £1 to average it out at $1.835. By the time it reached $1.825, I had buy bets worth £5. 'No problem,' I thought. 'It has fallen ten full cents now, so it is bound to rise. And anyway, I am unbeaten in nine trades in a row."

Again like you, Sally, I went on holiday to Penzance. When I came back, the exchange rate was $1.775, and I was staring at a loss of £2,500. I closed the trade.

"So all my hard work researching and successfully betting on things I never knew about before – what *is* a 30 year T bond? – went in a flash of the Arsenals. All because I was so determined to go through the whole year without losing one trade. (And because I failed to put on a stop-loss!)

"Three morals of my story:

1   Always put on a stop-loss.

2   You are never invincible – the little pixies at spread bettingland can turn nasty.

3   Never go to Penzance – it is obviously cursed."

This sad story inspires me to revisit the sterling/dollar charts. The trend is certainly down…all the way to $1.7395. I shared Andrew's view that it is destined to rise.

With the utmost confidence and the words, "Decide what you think will, for certain, happen, then trade precisely the opposite way" ringing with a Welsh lilt in my ears, I place a 50p sell bet.

Four winning trades later, plus two additional wins on the Dow and my confidence is restored. My Finspreads account currently stands at £2,002.

I'm back in the game.

Chapter Twenty-seven

I have nine winning trades. Does it really matter if we don't know what's driving the market?

September

Do you remember the Tamagotchi? It was the world's first virtual reality pet: a sophisticated toy that died of neglect unless you kept it fed, watered, nurtured and entertained. I am beginning to feel my adventures in spread betting are a latter-day version of this.

Sadly, my own personal 'Finagotchi' has suffered a nasty setback – one that could easily have been avoided had I been paying proper attention. Nothing fatal, but there was money sitting on the table just waiting to be siphoned into my account. Except I was otherwise occupied.

Guided by Supermum, I've narrowed my trading focus lately. So instead of buying and selling all over the place, I've been concentrating mostly on sterling/dollar exchange rate movements for the past couple of months.

Specialising pays off.

Nine of eleven recent trades have gone my way and I have a profit of over £500 to show for my endeavours!

I was beginning to feel I'd developed a real understanding for the rhythm of this market-that-never-sleeps. Cable and I were singing sweetly in tune.

So you can guess what happens next.

Next, I get the Opposite of Fan Mail from one of my regular correspondents, RW. Evidently, he hadn't been reading my blog, where I've been boasting about my gains.

"Dear veryunluckymoney," he begins. "I have written to you before, when I said that the trend is your friend, and that you should consider getting some decent software if you didn't have any. It can't be just bad luck that you keep losing these trades. I think you need to do some studying. Or give up."

This is the sort of lecture my Big Brother gives me from time to time.

Counterproductive.

I decide:

1   RW is being altogether too smug about his alleged regular wins on the Dow.

2   I have no wish to buy the software he recommends.

3   His advice can be safely ignored.

It is, therefore, inevitable, that my next trade is a duff one. I lose £279 when the dollar bucks the trend and weakens.

I confess that at this point, I sneak a look at RW's recommended software. The home page promises me a 'real edge' when trading the financial markets. Interestingly enough, it also enquires whether I would perform brain surgery with a plastic fork. And better even than this, the makers of this miracle short-cut to 'possibly millions' have incorporated astrology into their software system.

That's astrology as in Moon, Jupiter, Stars and Mars. Or as they themselves put it within an illustrated chart: 'Mercury and Venus set important price levels in this decline'.

A loser I might be, but frankly, I reckon anyone who parts with their money on the basis of this needs to have their head examined. With a plastic fork.

I often get emails asking me about charting software. It's big business. The net is packed with "Earn-£75k-Overnight" systems. Occasionally, they sound tempting. But at one financial seminar I attended, I met a man who'd bought SEVEN systems. The result? He was paralysed by information overload and conflicting advice and had yet to make a trade.

I digress.

My next two sterling/dollar trades – initiated by studying the charts rather than by waiting for a total eclipse of the sun – recaptured £112.

It's time for my next tutorial with Supermum and I begin with an obvious question. "What's driving the £/$ market?"

Supermum feeds her youngest a croissant and considers. "The dollar trades on US economic data. It's all down to the numbers," she says. "There's NAPAM – that's the National Association of

Production Managers – then there's the trade deficit, CPI, PPI, Beige Books, Red Books, Jobs Numbers, the Non Farm Payroll. Oh, and the interest rates."

I point out that so far, this is all about words and letters, rather than numbers. "I so don't get it. Are they meant to be going up? Or down?"

"Listen." Supermum's kindly voice reminds me of a teacher who has decided a student is heading for deferred success, and is more suited to a lower set. "Forget everything I just said. For the moment, at least. What really drives the dollar is the price of oil."

I didn't have to wait long to see what Supermum meant. Hurricane Katrina devastated New Orleans... oil prices rocketed in response.... and the dollar declined against the pound by almost six cents in a couple of days.

Six hundred points available from Finspreads to anyone who hit the buy button at the right moment.

As it so happened, this mayhem coincided with my birthday. I was nowhere near a computer, and trading was the last thing on my mind.

Sally Nicoll's Unique Market Insight #1:

> *This brings me full circle to the Tamagotchi: the moment you take your eye off the market is inevitably the moment when there's money to be made.*

I try to learn from my mistakes. So when Hurricane Rita begins her flight path to Texas, I am sitting at my trading screen.

Sure enough, oil prices rise. But the dollar? Mysteriously, it has strengthened by five cents.

"What's going on?" I ask Supermum.

"Buggered if I know." Fortunately, the kids are not around to hear their mother's professional verdict. "But don't worry about it. Go with the trend."

An hour later, Supermum phones. "I've been talking to a friend in Boston," she says. "They think it's the Chinese. They've had enough of Treasury bonds and are accumulating currency in a big way."

The moral of this piece of hot gossip?

The way I see it, the forces that move the market are, to a greater extent, irrelevant. And although it is certainly comforting when you think you understand what's going on, what really matters is to follow the trend. And as Supermum repeats frequently, "Trade what you see. Not what you think."

Oh, and if you're trading in a seriously volatile market like Cable, think Tamagotchi.

Now, should I sell? Or wait for the market to recover?

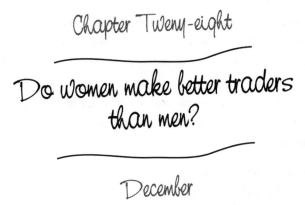

Chapter Twenty-eight

Do women make better traders than men?

December

It's lonely in Primrose Hill. Retired Reggie sends me emails from Hungary, where he's enjoying a whole new lease of life. Much Divorced Michael seems to have vanished from the scene. And my Great Uncle Gareth has died. It wasn't unexpected, but that doesn't make it any less sad.

At the funeral, I am surrounded by well-meaning relatives, asking me when my novel will be appearing. This has the effect of making me take my fiction more seriously. It helps that we're now deep into a London winter. It's raining all the time, and even Dow-Wow reckons twenty-minutes in the park is more than enough. I've arrived at chapter thirty-one, with more than 80,000 words down on paper. It's all starting to go very pear-shaped for the villain, but he's fighting back better than I'd imagined. And the next few chapters – involving a HUGE MI5 sting – take place right here in Primrose Hill. Just as soon as I've done my research about helicopters and tracking devices.

Meanwhile, I've been making the headlines, too. In a minor way. I've been interviewed by Finspreads for their customer newsletter. The article is about the growing popularity of spread betting amongst women – five years ago there were only six female account holders, but we'll soon account for ten per cent of the client base. It goes so far as to suggest that women make better traders than blokes.

According to Sheila Gleason, Marketing Operations Director within Barclays Wealth Management, "There are distinct differences between the trading styles of men and women. Quite simply, when it comes to trading, the genders are influenced by different emotions."

What are the differences?

MEN

- Focused on results

- Goal directed

- Single-minded in their approach

- Risk tolerant

- Centred on fact-based assessment

- Often over-confident

WOMEN

- Multi-focused

- Process directed

- Less driven than men

- Safety conscious and conservative

- Intuitive – sensitive to a variety of information

- Less prone to over-confidence

Women who trade successfully with Finspreads are featured. One of them asserts, "I know everyone says there are plenty of losing traders, but on average I expect to win. When I do lose, it's usually because I've been lazy and haven't spent enough time planning my strategy. Although having said that, I'm definitely not the type of trader who spends hours staring at the screen – life's too short."

By contrast, I am described as 'a clown fish swimming innocently amongst the sharks'.

As if that weren't bad enough, when I use my initiative to contact the successful trader, she gives me a right bollocking. "Women like you give women like me a bad name," she declares. "Isn't it time you started taking it seriously?"

And a Merry Christmas to you, too.

Chapter Twenty-nine

My New Year Trading Plan
And tragic news about the
Google share price

January 2006

My New Year Resolutions:

1   Finish my novel

2   Acquire a literary agent

3   Try internet dating

4   Take spread betting more seriously

5   Drink less coffee

It's three weeks later. How am I doing?

Resolution No 5 fell by the wayside pretty early on. I blame Retired Reggie. He's back from Hungary, having completed his contract. Presumably, the fashionistas of Budapest are now swaggering around looking like Twiggy, Erin, Laura and that other model in the Marks and Spencer ads, the one whose name no-one ever remembers.

As for Much Divorced Michael, he's reappeared too, accompanied by a dog the size of a Shetland Pony. It looks like Tossa, but it can't possibly be her. Far too well behaved. Sits on command. Offers a paw the size of Mike Tyson's fist. Even tolerates having a biscuit balanced on the end of her nose until Michael gives permission for her to eat it. Dow Jones takes fright and hides behind my legs.

"Father Christmas give you a set of tranquiliser darts?" Reggie enquires.

"Remember those puppy training classes," Michael replies. "We ended up going on the intensive course."

Reggie cottons on before I do. "What's her name?"

"Julia."

Michael sounds like a man in love. Apparently Julia lives in Sevenoaks. Geographically unsuitable, if you ask me. But distance has proved no barrier for this man and his dog. It's sounding serious – just like every romance Michael ever embarks on.

I ponder my own romantic initiatives. I've signed up for a couple of internet dating sites. Been inundated with emails, which is good for the ego. But have yet to venture out on a date.

The novel continues to go well. I'm nearly finished. But the strangest thing has happened. The other night, I'm dining with Supermum in our local Greek restaurant. Just as I'm trying to get my pork kebab off the skewer without skidding the chunks of meat across the tablecloth as I usually do, a lone diner walks in.

Blimey! It's one of my characters. Lord Robert Dunstan. He's come to life and is sitting at the next table. A giant of a man, whose head seems too small for the rest of him. Malevolent blue eyes. Fists the size of hams, and hands that have never experienced physical labour. The expensive, but ill-fitting suit that he still wears because he refuses to acknowledge his thickened waistline. And an aura of self-importance that you can spot at twenty paces.

All exactly as I have described. Naturally, I can't resist the opportunity to talk to the guy. Not that I have to say much; just like my character Dunstan, the gentleman in question needs little encouragement to flaunt both his opinions and his prejudices.

He drones on while we finish our supper, and looks mildly put out when I advise him to drive safely. Only trying to help – I know what fate has in store for Dunstan…

Supermum thinks I'm working too hard. She's given me a few more spread betting mentoring sessions, and has been getting me to paper trade for the past few weeks..

I have a new, improved strategy for 2006:

'Sally Nicoll's New Improved Strategy (2006)'

Get rich slow

Here's the plan for successful spread betting:

1. I'm going to take it all more seriously
Do my homework. Scope out markets that offer the best chance of success. Only enter trades when I have a good reason. And stop holding losing positions at all costs when my only justification is that I am a foolishly optimistic Type A personality.

2. I'm abandoning my previous focus on sterling/dollar trading

Have come to the conclusion that when you put all your eggs into a single basket of currencies, you're most likely to get boiled, scrambled, poached and fried.

3. From now on, I want to be a position trader

In other words, hang on to my trades for at least a few days and hopefully longer. I want to become less gambler and more investor. After all, I've made money out of buying stocks and shares in the past. No reason why I shouldn't do so again.

4. I'm not going to use software packages that purport to tell me when to buy and sell

As well as the asking-me-out emails, I've had tons of Finspreads customers discussing the value of the various packages they use. My conclusion is that they all seem like an expensive way to line the pockets of others. PB, a portfolio manager who's in charge of $2billion worth of assets solved my should-I try-one dilemma with an email that advised: "Don't believe in charts and software. Instead, I stick to fundamentals and behavioural finance, which recognises that emotions like regret, pride, overconfidence, snakebite (once bitten twice shy), fear of loss and greed often lead to poor investment decisions. Behavioural finance concludes that investors are irrational and are loss averse rather than risk averse. This can lead them to trade or not to trade, in order to avoid losses – hold a losing position at all costs and with disregard to whether their original justification for putting on the trade still exists." I empathise with most of this, and spend the afternoon Googling "behavioural finance". Then I make the mistake of Googling Google's share price. It's currently around $400 – more than DOUBLE the price of a year ago. I do some back-of-an-envelope calculations. An increase of $275... that translates to 27,500 points… 50p buy trade… isn't that £10,750? Just by going with the trend?

SO WHY HADN'T I JUST STUCK TO GOOGLE??

I spend the rest of the day Googling cures for depression.

Chapter Thirty

I do well enough to start dreaming about villas in the South of France – and a yacht

The End of January

Back to that paper trading experiment.

Once I confined myself to placing hypothetical trades, I inevitably clocked-up excellent make-believe profits. I concentrated mostly on one particular share: CSR, a mid-cap stock that I'd read about in the Sunday papers. The company is based in Cambridge and, according to their web site, are world leaders in Bluetooth connectivity.

I've written the words for a few web sites in my time, and know only too well how easily copywriters can get carried away. So I decided to investigate further. CSR, according to independent sources, do business with the likes of Nokia, Dell, Motorola, IBM, Sony and more.

Good enough for me.

I built an imaginary position of £5 a point (five separate hypothetical trades of 50p, £2, 50p, £1, £1 respectively) and watched the share climb from 900 to 1100 during December.

My buying strategy? Yes, I actually had one! Nothing complicated:

- I'd sit smugly watching the price go up.

- And then up some more.

- Eventually, of course, there'd be a pullback.

- No sweat.

- No selling of my winning trade.

- I'd sit smugly watching the price go down.

- Eventually, of course, the price would start to rise again.

- And THAT'S when I'd smugly buy some more.

Why oh why hadn't I done this with Google?

Enough remorse. Can I make this work with real money? With my Finspreads account £1,800 in credit, it's certainly time to try. So last week, I started stalking CSR for real, and on Thursday I decided it was time to buy. Not because any charting software issued a buy signal, but because I read (via Google News) that CSR is now producing some gizmo that lets you Bluetooth your iPod to a home stereo. Without further ado, I placed my trade: 50p buy of the March contract at a price of 1088.7.

Fast forward to the following morning.

I log on, and CSR has gapped up – opened much higher than it closed the previous day – and has already raced 100 points ahead.

Given my old strategy, I'd have taken my profits at once. But not any more! I sit back and watch the price continue to soar. It adds a further 50 points, before dropping back in the final hour of trading.

Today, exactly as I expected, CSR has pulled back. My trade, which was worth more than £70 at one point, is currently £39.30 in profit. Am I disappointed? Put it this way: I've gleefully bought another £1 of the March contract. Right this moment, the trade is £11 down.

Bothered? Do I look bothered?

And you haven't heard the half of it yet!

About ten days ago, what's now emerging as the Livedoor Scandal rocked the markets in Japan. (Livedoor's a technology company and has been a stock market superstar – until now.) Sensing an opportunity, I checked out the chart for the Nikkei 225. Rather like CSR, it had been doing one of those beautiful up-and-up-and-up lines. Until now. It had fallen six per cent in two days – a BIG dip.

"Which means," I said to myself, "There's scope for it to gain a thousand points or so, when it recovers. Let's roll!"

I forced myself to do some research before I got stuck in. The collective online financial wisdom declared Livedoor was more Martha Stewart than Enron, so I placed a: 50p buy trade with the index at 15,413. Having done this, I did some further research, only to discover the news sources were now predicting a third day of heavy falls.

Which is how I come to be in front of my computer at midnight – Finspreads, like the old Windmill Theatre, never closes and it's now open 24/7 – flicking between Bloomberg and Celebrity Big Brother

Live, while I wait for the Tokyo stock exchange to open. A Japanese commentator is busily talking up the market: he's not as entertaining as Preston and Chantelle, but he definitely gets my vote.

What a night!

My trade soars faster than a bullet train. I lose my nerve just as it's getting light. The index is now 15,645, and I close my trade for a profit of £116.

Sally Nicoll's Market Insight #2:

> *Spread betting. This is the way I always dreamed it could be. It's so much fun when you're winning.*

There's no pause in the rally, so I buy back in at 15,730.

Guess what?

There's been another huge rise when I check my account the following morning. I have finally discovered the secret of making money when I sleep.

This time I let my profits continue to run until teatime, when they reach a magnificent £350. I close my trade with a flourish, only because I don't want to risk giving back the money if something bad happens over the weekend.

But I'm not completely out of the market. Remember, I'm a position trader now. So as well as my £1.50 CSR trades I still have the following in play:

1. £1 buy FTSE100 March @ 5665
This was, in fact, my first trade of the year, back in mid-January. I'm hoping we'll pass the 6000 mark, and I'm currently showing a

profit of £108.

2. 50p buy Brent Crude March @ 65.86

I went into this trade a day too late – once a big leap had already happened because of worries about oil supplies in Nigeria and Iran – and it's been yo-yoing up and down for a week. Since OPEC output is now expected to remain unchanged, I've just this minute cut and run for a loss of £4.50.

3. TWO £1 trades on the WIG MARCH @ 2970 and 2965

This has nothing to do with hairpieces. It's down to an email from a Finspreads reader, Mike K, who drew my attention to the merits of Poland's equivalent of the FTSE. Poland's economy is booming, and the WIG has gone from 1800 to 3000 in a year, without any major reversals. So I have high hopes of this one. That's why I increased my stake, buying some more at a better price. Strongly tempted to keep buying, too. But since the WIG's been pulling back for three days, I'm biding my time, and waiting until both trades show a clear profit.

So what's the bottom line? I have banked two winning Japan trades and my modest oil loser for a total profit of £461.50. So there is now £2,146.48 in my Finspreads account. And my open Profit and Loss on the open FTSE and WIG trades is currently £91.55.

I reported my progress to Supermum with, as you will understand, particular emphasis on my Japanese exploits.

She gave me a long, level look. "So you've been dreaming about villas in the South of France and a yacht, have you?"

That woman's a mind reader!

Chapter Thirty-one

Pride comes before a fall

March

Hard times here in Primrose Hill. Retired Reggie is missing his Hungarian consultancy fees. Michael is thinking of proposing to Julia, so we assume he's started to save for his next divorce. As for me...

Let's talk about something else.

I've been entertaining my dearest friends with Tales of Internet Dating. There have been three so far:

Internet date #1
Take it from me, Starbucks in Golders Green is not the ideal venue for a romantic first date. Felix K claimed to be a publisher. (So why shouldn't I mix business with pleasure?) If he publishes anything, I reckon it's a magazine for serial killers. I sent an emergency text to Supermum and she came to rescue me in her getaway car. Didn't even make my excuses and leave. I just fled.

Internet date #2

His name was Maxwell and he was gorgeous. One of my older men, this one in his forties, with delicious salt and pepper hair. We met in Chinatown. I thought we were having dinner, but after we'd had a couple of drinks, HE got an emergency text...

Internet date #3

Julian. Who should have been spending the evening with Much Divorced Michael, rather than me. I listened for three hours while he droned on about his two ex-wives, the three children he's not allowed to see and his failing IT business. Supermum wasn't answering her phone, so I was obliged to stay for dessert. I reached for my purse, eager to pay my share of the bill, so that I wouldn't be under any sense of obligation. "Oh, are you paying for me? That's very kind. My treat next time!" As we parted, I stood well away, so he couldn't make a sudden lunge. But somehow I ended up in a clammy embrace. "There's something I have to tell you," he whispered wetly into my ear. "I'm having my haemorrhoids surgically removed next week."

Michael and Reggie think I'm making that last one up, but I'm afraid it's all horribly true.

And if you think my love life's dire, just wait until you hear about my spread betting.

I sat down to write my final blog for Finspreads. My financial obituary. After two years of trading – doing it very much My Way – I was planning to mention my few regrets (principally, that I don't have enough winning trades) and then slink away.

Until...

Before I tell you what's happened, we need to go back to those open trades of mine. The ones I was so sure would continue my start-of-the-year winning streak.

First off, my plan to invade Poland via their WIG Index was going horribly wrong. I wanted to trade the WIG because my great-grandmother came from Gdansk (this is not what they mean by market sentiment, I know, I know) and because Ula, our favourite waitress at J's, who comes from Krakow, is always telling us her home-country economy is going from strength to strength. The WIG chart echoed her verdict – it just goes up and up – so my two £1 buy trades would rival the two I'd kept open on CSR.

Which they duly did. Although not as I had hoped.

The WIG dropped 120 points within a matter of hours. What had gone wrong? Nothing Polish showed up in the BBC headlines, so I did a frantic Google.

My search led me to a mournful report. The Polish press was already referring to its stockmarket nosedive as Black Tuesday. Apparently, the meltdown had been triggered by a copper producing company called KGHM.

KGHM makes up 19% of the WIG, and had self-combusted – assuming copper can self-combust – by a monumental 12.6% in a single trading session. Its collapse had prompted Polish stockholders the world over to sell, sell, SELLLLLLLLL!

Trading volumes had been the fourth highest in the history of the Warsaw Stock Exchange, I discovered. I also learned the Polish word for February is "Lutego". Neither piece of information offered much consolation.

"You are a position trader," I sternly reminded myself. "This is a setback. Nothing more. Might even represent an excellent buying opportunity."

In the time it took me to ponder an additional £3 a point trade, the WIG continued to decline. I took my finger off the buy button. This turned out to be a smart decision, because by the time they closed for business in Warsaw, I would have been an additional £105 down.

At least my adventures in Japan had been more successful. Right?

Alas, not. I lost £486.50 when the Nikkei declined from 16,583 to 15,610 and my March contract expired. I'd been hanging on, confident of recovery. Which duly happened a few days later. Unfortunately, I was still licking my wounds. When what I should have been doing was buying back into a rising market. Ironically enough, the amount I lost was almost exactly the same as I had won back in January.

I consoled myself by taking profits of £175.5 on two FTSE trades.

By this time, my remaining trades were lurching towards their own March expiry dates. CSR had long since failed to live up to its earlier star status. And in Poland, there continued to be more sellers than buyers.

I was almost relieved when the Finspreads system automatically closed my trades. I'd taken a serious hammering: total losses of £462 on the WIG and CSR. (Can you feel me wince as I write that last sentence?)

I'd finally had enough. Time for me to fold my calculator and bid farewell to Finspreads while I still had £1,400 left in my account.

Better to finish the final few chapters of my novel and concentrate instead on finding a literary agent to make me rich. My final blog was the saddest story since Black Beauty.

Fortunately, I never had the chance to post it. Because then the letter arrived.

From the lawyer.

Chapter Thirty-two

I am commanded from beyond the grave to continue my trading education

One Week Later

You remember my Great Uncle Gareth, who died just before Christmas. It's his lawyer who's written to me. Says he needs to come and see me. Urgently. The fact it's this way round, rather than a summons to his office, fills me with foreboding. I'd always thought those student hand-outs were gifts. Am I supposed to pay them back into his estate, or what?

I spend a frantic morning tidying the flat, grooming Dow Jones and going through my financial paperwork. It's not quite a disaster. I can finish the novel in a month, start touting for advertising work again, and there's still a few bob left in my Finspreads account, if the lawyer wants money from me right away.

He arrives just as I finish removing dog hair from the couch. A man in his fifties, wearing a sharp suit and a pair of Himmler spectacles. Looks a bit like Jeffrey Archer. I fuss around making coffee and polite conversation. The weather. Tottenham's chances of finishing above the Gooners. Gordon Brown's chances of succeeding Tony Blair. But eventually, it's time for business, and in the finest of traditions, I am invited to take a seat – in my own home!

Before we go any further, let me just fill you in on Great Uncle Gareth. GUG, as he was known to the family, lived a long, happy and apparently blameless life. We all thought the most out-of-character thing he ever did was the sponsored sky-dive on his 78th birthday. He used to be a quantity surveyor. After which, he kept himself busy – as they say – for the better part of three decades.

But only now do I discover exactly how industrious he'd been.

GUG, it turns out, had been keeping himself extraordinarily busy. Not with Sudoku puzzles… or tea dances… or even gardening. Nope. At the grand old age of ninety-one, GUG was, according to this lawyer, still putting in eight-hour days on the computer. Managing his enormous portfolio of shares and other investments.

He was bloody good at it, too. GUG was a whole lot richer than any of us ever imagined. Think seven figures. And think again if you imagined the first figure was a one.

While he certainly never lived a life of poverty, GUG never gave the impression of wealth, either. As I say, he helped me out when I was at Uni, which was generous. In time, I was able to reciprocate a bit – and in retrospect, how GUG must have chuckled when I gave him Marks and Spencer vouchers on his birthday. Firstly, because I made a big deal about wanting to treat him to some posh nosh. And then again because of the shedloads of M&S shares he'd accumulated over the years.

The lawyer knew him really well. They'd met through an investment club somewhere out near Monmouth. I learn that GUG had an entirely different nickname amongst his fellow-investors, though. They called him Midas.

I expect by now, you think you know where this story is going. That GUG has left me his entire fortune. That yours truly has scooped that jackpot and is now a millionairess.

Well, yes, and no.

I have been given an astonishingly generous legacy... but it's more like three oranges appearing in a straight line on the fruit machine, as opposed to three heavy sacks of cash.

Among other things I've learned today is that GUG followed my adventures with Finspreads with keen interest. Never missed a report. I gather I am also a source of great amusement to the Monmouth Investors Club.

GUG admired:

- My tenacity: "'You never seem to know when you're beaten!' as the Jeffrey Archer look-a-like puts it."

- My honesty: "Maybe it's a gender thing, that women admit their mistakes more easily than men do?"

- My willingness to put my money on the line: "Gareth liked the fact that you never moaned about your losses."

All this praise. It's got me blushing and weeping at the same time. How on earth am I going to tell Jeffrey Archer I've decided trading is not for me. In the end, I just blurt it out.

"But you've put in all this work!" GUG's lawyer responds. "Almost every successful trader goes through a learning curve. True, you've lost money. But you're aware of the mistakes you've made. So it would be a shame to give up now. And besides, Gareth was very keen that you should continue."

So now let me tell you what GUG has done.

Quite apart from the generous legacy, I've been offered an additional £20,000. But there are strings. If I accept the extra cash, I must pay it into my Finspreads account and use it – as he put it – to continue my trading education.

What would you have done?

I ask what will happen to the £20k if I decline. Can I give the lot to charity? Or bet the lot on Arsenal to lose in the Champions League Final? Or even stick it in some unit trusts?

No! NO! And Definitely NOT! Finspreads or nothing. Except – a reproachful look from Jeffrey Archer – GUG would have been extremely disappointed if I fail to rise to the challenge, and the money disappears into the residue of the estate.

No emotional blackmail there, then.

Chapter Thirty-three

I finally get the hang of spread betting And make nineteen successive winning trades

May

After the lawyer had left I just sat there for hours, staring at the wall. Part of me still thought this was a practical joke, and that Chris Tarrant was about to appear – accompanied by television cameras – and tell me I was the victim of some Candid Camera remake.

Then I got a phone call from Big Brother. He was equally gobsmacked by GUG's outrageous generosity. That made me feel a lot better – at least I hadn't been singled out for unfair treatment. Except, of course, Big Brother was under no obligation to spread bet. Which was just as well, since he wouldn't know a September futures contract from a hole in the ground.

One thing seemed certain. These pennies from heaven meant I could pay off the mortgage and spend another couple of years trying to make it as a novelist. And Dow Jones could have the sparkly collar I'd been coveting in the pet shop window for the past few weeks.

A few days later, when I blogged on Finspreads about GUG's legacy, my inbox almost collapsed under the weight of email. Sixteen hard-luck stories asking me to share my luck. Three proposals of marriage. Several proposals that clearly did NOT include marriage. And many genuinely nice messages of congratulations.

Talking of nuptials, Much Divorced Michael and Julia the Dog Whisperer are engaged! He's drawn the line at moving to Sevenoaks, so the canine fraternity of Primrose Hill had better be on guard: Tossa is a shadow of her former self, so well behaved she's a giant Stepford Dog – all sit, stay, give us your paw, and roll over. She even chews her croissants as daintily as any seven-stone creature can, instead of swallowing them whole, as she used to.

"This spread betting thing," says Retired Reggie the other morning. "Does it feel any different now your account's got so much money in it?"

Before I can answer, a man in uniform marches up to our table. "Are you Sally Nicoll?" he barks.

My first thought is that Camden have finally come to arrest me for that crack I made about the Stud Nazis. Either that or I must have forgotten to pay a parking ticket. Before I can ask Reggie to bring Dow-Wow to visit me in Holloway, the uniform consults his notebook. "You complained to us about recycling."

Indeed, I had. Camden Council has issued me with a large brown plastic box for newspaper recycling. Great idea. Except that when it's full, it weighs a ton, and I can't lift it from my basement to the street for collection. Hence, it doesn't get collected.

"Our environmental operatives are unable to go up and down

stairs," the uniform continues. "Health and safety."

Retired Reggie chokes on his Americano. "Isn't that like saying fire operatives are unable to go anywhere hot?" he enquires.

Uniform ignores him and addresses me, instead. "However, we have decided to issue you with a disabled recycling box."

I know Reggie is about to ask whether than means the box is in a wheelchair, so I speak before he can. "Thank you," I mutter.

When I get home, I find a box with fat strips of red and white reflective tape attached to its lid. With luck, the Council now has me on some list of the 'challenged' and will soon send me a coveted disabled parking badge. Or offer me a job as a fire operative.

Anyway. This spread betting thing.

It's been extremely weird, the impact of GUG's legacy. I'm still trading within my own rules: this is money I *can* afford to lose, although naturally, I am keen to make it grow. But now I feel obliged to be more responsible in my trades.

As if that's not weird enough, something even stranger has happened. The moment I began trading with GUG's money, I started to win.

In fact, I can't STOP winning!

I have made NINETEEN successive winning trades.

Let's just pause for a moment and contemplate…

HOW AWESOME IS THAT??????!

…

Fully contemplated?

OK, we'll move on.

Twelve of these wins have come from the zigging and zagging of the FTSE. I've realised that while it never goes much over 6100, neither does it fall much under 5970. So if I buy after a steep fall – anything over 50 points in a session is enough to make me smile broadly – and then sell once it's heading up again, I can't go wrong.

I'm still being cautious with my stakes: mostly £1 trades, and then I buy some more when I'm in profit.

- My biggest win's been on the FTSE May contract – I collected £136 for a £2 trade.

- My average FTSE profit is £62 per trade.

- I've also made £168.19 on two NIFTY trades. The NIFTY is India's FTSE, and as the Indian economy races ahead, their stock market has doubled in the past two years.

- The WIG's going from strength to strength again, as well, and I made £191.50 on my buy trade.

- Gold has also been reaching record prices of over $700 dollars an ounce. More buying opportunities and I've made £141.50 on my trades.

I've won a total of £1,259.28. That's a 6% return on GUG's legacy.

It feels like he's guiding my trading choices.

Chapter Thirty-four

Pride comes before a fall (Part II)

June

We're discussing the forthcoming divorce of Paul and Heather McCartney.

Reggie and Michael think it's outrageous that the soon-to-be-ex-Lady McCartney is holding out for a meaty chunk of Paul's wealth. I'm remembering the cute toddler who stroked Dow-Wow right here in J's…

"You've got a soft spot for Paul, haven't you Sally?" Reggie teases me. "He's only a few years younger than me. Does that mean I'm in with a chance, too? How's your internet dating coming along?"

I've packed it in. Turned up on a blind date only to find the man who sounded so good on paper had arrived with his ex-girlfriend in tow. Enough to put anyone off for life.

Much Divorced Michael is wondering how to broach the tricky subject of a pre-nuptial agreement with Julia the Dog Whisperer.

While Reggie reveals he is setting up his own website, advertising his services as a fashion designer.

I'm about to make my excuses and leave – it is, after all, gone ten o'clock and I am on the penultimate chapter of my novel – when an old friend approaches our table.

Don the Drug Dealer – sorry pharmaceutical sales executive – is looking great. Casually yet expensively dressed. And that's a vintage Rolex on his wrist.

"Sally!" he seems genuinely pleased to see me.

"Where've you been?"

"I've moved to France. Packed in the job. And it's all thanks to you!"

I allow Don to buy me another latte.

Guess what?

He's taken up spread betting.

Full-time.

And he's really, really, good at it.

"How's your trading going?" he asks after a while. "Made enough to move into St George's Terrace? I remember you've always fancied a place with a view of the park."

My trading.

A disaster. Total disaster.

The markets began to take a dive during the second week of May. I had carried on buying. And buying. And then some.

With nineteen successive winning trades, and GUG's celestial guiding hand, how could I go wrong?

It wasn't just the FTSE that was in freefall.

The Nikkei.

The NIFTY.

The WIG.

Even gold.

Especially gold.

In meltdown.

All of them.

"You alright, Sally?" asks Michael. "You've gone terribly pale."

The truth is that I've lost almost £4,000.

And I'm too ashamed to tell anyone.

There's worse to follow.

I've had an email from someone called Stephen Eckett. Says he's the commissioning editor for a financial publisher. Claims to be a big fan of my Finspreads pieces. Reckons they'd make a great book.

I guess they can call it *The Idiot's Guide To Spread Betting*.

Chapter Thirty-five

Sensible advice from a man who lost $10m – in a single day

One Week Later

One of my dad's favourite sporting stories was about this bloke called Maurice Flitcroft. It was back in the dark ages – I was still knee-high to a pinball machine – when, armed with a half-set of clubs he'd bought from a mail order catalogue and an instructional library book, Mr Flitcroft paid £30 to enter British golf's premier tournament: The Open Championships.

His round was described by a sports journalist as a 'blizzard of triple and quadruple bogeys ruined by a solitary par', and his score of 121 – 49 over par – will forever remain the worst in the tournament's history.

Afterwards, Mr Flitcroft commented, "I expected to do reasonably well. But in spite of all that practising, I hadn't progressed as much as I would have liked."

The story, and my dad's telling of it, came back to me when my contract from the publishing people arrived. A published author.

Isn't that everyone's ambition? When *The Guardian* upgraded their servers last year, a total of 243 novels-in-progress were discovered in the system. Allegedly.

I had dreamed of being published for three years.

Never like this though.

My book was meant to keep company with the likes of Robert Ludlum, John Grisham and David Baldacci.

But my adventures in spread betting are pure Stephen King.

"This is like Anne Diamond and her diet books," I complain to Michael and Reggie. "Or Maurice Flitcroft."

"Is he our local councillor?" asks Reggie.

I tell my dad's story, although not as well as he would have done.

"You don't fancy being a magnificent failure, then?" Michael summarises. "Only one thing for it, Sally," his voice is suddenly serious. "You're going to have to learn how to win."

This is good advice. Until now, I have been trying to gatecrash the elite world of City traders equipped with the equivalent of tools from Argos. The moment I get back to my computer, I email Sandy Jadeja, who is now chief market analyst with Finspreads. "Remember me?" I begin. "Incredible as it may seem, a publisher called Harriman House want to publish a version of my trading blog. So I need to become a better trader. Fast. I see you're running one of your courses on Saturday. Is there room for me to attend?"

Sandy evidently does remember me. He responds, "Sorry Sally. The course is full up."

Undeterred, I plead, "Can I go on the reserve list, in case someone drops out?"

"No-one will drop out."

"Well how about if I come and hand out the tea and biscuits?"

"The hotel is very strict about how many people attend. Health and Safety regulations."

From this email exchange, I conclude that Sandy thinks I am beyond redemption, and doesn't want his reputation sullied by my catalogue of failure.

What next?

Warren Buffet doesn't reply to either of the emails I send him.

But how about my friend Mads? That's pronounced Mass, by the way. Danish. I've known him for years. He'd been a hugely successful bond dealer – good enough to take a break from the City in his early thirties to spend more time with his kids.

Last year's Christmas card had come from Hong Kong. I'm delighted when his email response arrives from Mayfair. And a day later, I'm in the offices of the hedge fund where Mads is now employed.

Hedge funds.

They've been around for over fifty years. The big idea was to sell short some stocks, while buying others – so that some of the market risk was hedged.

If this sounds a touch familiar, you're right. Hedge funds are spread betting on a grand scale. I learn:

- There are about 9000 funds worldwide.

- It's common for a hedge fund investor to control $100million in securities with a down payment of just $5 million.

- Last year, the world's top 25 hedge fund managers earned an average of $251,000,000 – each.

And – most pertinent of all – it's entirely because of people like my pal Mads that my NIFTY May futures trades went sour. The hedge fund boys have been piling into India, looking for big returns. They've invested using billions of dollars, borrowed cheaply, while interest rates were low. But on 11th May, the US Federal Reserve raised interest rates, and hinted at further increases to come.

Result?

- The professionals pulled their trades.

- The NIFTY plummeted 25%.

- I lost £468.25.

"Sorry about that," says Mads. "Let's see if I can help make it up to you."

His offices reek of posh money. Understated elegance. On the desk, sit the tools of Mads' trade. Four Bloomberg screens that definitely didn't come from a mail order catalogue. Each screen subdivides into a series of brightly coloured rectangles – mostly containing charts and market prices – at a quick glance, you'd take them for modern works of art.

The biggest plasma screen I've ever seen is tuned to CNN. On another wall there's what looks like an airport arrivals board. It flashes red and green signals whenever there's a change in the price of gold, oil and other commodities.

I also notice the signed photo of an Arsenal player on another wall, but this is no time to quibble. Reluctantly, I show Mads my trading history. I see him trying to control a flinch, but when he speaks, his voice is kind.

"You've been running your losses and cutting your profits," he announces. "That's not uncommon when you're inexperienced."

Mads offers me a cup of coffee. In the kitchen, I notice he's pouring bottled Evian into the machine. This is the most conspicuous consumption I've experienced since the last advertising boom, when our office receptionist insisted on watering the plants with Perrier. I try not to laugh.

We go back into the main office and Mads switches back to his Bloomberg screens. "Are you using moving averages?" he asks.

Moving averages.

I'd forgotten all about them.

Moving averages help you spot trends. They're as useful to traders as full stops are to writers. Unlike full stops, however, they come in a variety of shapes and sizes. For example, there's the ten-day moving average. You get this by adding up the closing prices of – say – the FTSE from the past ten days, and then dividing the result by ten. Fortunately, you don't have to do the sums; you just select the moving average you want from the menu of indicators and it automatically appears, overlaid on your chart.

"I generally use moving averages for 200 days, 20 days and 5 days,"

Mads confides. "To see the short-term, medium and long-term trend." A few clicks and all three indicators appear on his FTSE chart: red, orange and green wavy lines. Now even I can see that in May, when the FTSE crashed, the chart fell below the moving averages. More to the point, I understand that if I want to trade right this minute, I'll be more likely to win if I sell rather than buy – because the indicators clearly show the FTSE is trending down in both the short and the medium-term.

This is probably my most interesting discovery since I realised I could read.

There's more.

Mads starts adding trend lines to his chart. They shoot across the screen like neon lasers. Next, he reminds me about support and resistance. I'd got the hang of this earlier, when I was doing so well with my own FTSE trades. Remember – the index was trading between about 6100 and 5970:

- Resistance: 6100 (the market resisted going any higher).

- Support: 5970 (the market supported the price from going any lower).

Twenty-twenty hindsight is always so enlightening. I should have accepted my losses and switched to selling as soon as it was clear the FTSE was below 5970. Whereas, I'd carried on buying, like I was at the Selfridges sale on opening day.

Other top tips from Mads:

- Think about Event Trading. Say the Bank of England or the Federal Reserve is making an interest rate announcement at

11.30am. Sit and monitor the FTSE, or the Dow. The market will react the moment the news comes through. If rates go up, people sell. The opposite if they fall. Basically, just follow the money!

- Fridays are often volatile trading days, because that's when fund managers are executing their strategies.

- Commodities just seem to go up and up…

- The Asian economy looks more promising than Europe or America right now.

I also talk to Mads about his own trading – and I'm surprised at the answers.

His hedge fund has $30 million under management – that makes it relatively small – and it aims to make a profit of 1% a month, which compounds to 15% a year. He works with three colleagues, and between them they open or close an average of only 3 trades a day. On the day I visited, there were 15 open trades.

"I lose about 45% of my trades," says Mads.

"What's the most you've ever lost?"

"Ten million dollars. In a day. On a fixed income trade."

Mads is so casual. It's as if he's talking about a fiver he lost in the street. I feel better about my own recent disasters. "What about the most you've ever won?"

"About the same." He's equally matter-of-fact.

"Anything else I should know?"

"Never bet more than you can afford to lose."

My dad would have liked Mads.

As I prepare to leave, Mads returns to the Finspreads web site. "I like their trading platform," he comments. "Tell me. What's the maximum I can trade per point?"

There's a certain glint in his eye...

Chapter Thirty-six

My spread betting secret is out!

That Weekend

I have signed on the dotted line, and am now contractually obliged to produce a book on spread betting. This has had the effect of inspiring me to spend the rest of the week finishing my real book – my novel. I write as fast as I can, and pause only to take Dow Jones to the park.

As Friday turns into Saturday, I am finally ready to hit the print key.

Four hundred and twenty five pages. Either I have a novel. Or a lot of typing.

One book down, and one to go.

Completing your first manuscript is a cause for celebration. And in my case, someone else is throwing the party. Much Divorced Michael and Julia the Dog Whisperer are tying the knot.

Considering he's done this so many times before, you'd think

Michael would be a laid-back bridegroom. Not a bit of it. He's fussing around, making sure Reggie hasn't lost the ring... that Tossa is wearing her matching new pink collar and lead... and most important of all, that Julia's parents remain blissfully unaware he's in possession of more than one divorce absolute.

"You are NOT to say 'Welcome Back' or 'Here We Are Again' when you make the speech," he insists to Retired Reggie.

In the event, it all goes smoothly.

At least until the reception.

"I'm so looking forward to Venice," Julia tells me. "Always wanted to go there." She's watching my face carefully. "Don't worry." she grins. "I know all about Michael and Venice."

Is this woman a saint?

"Men are like dogs, Sally," she confides. "They thrive on routine. Michael's good at Venice. Knows his way around. And the Cipriani says Tossa is welcome to share the Dogaressa suite with us. Appropriate, isn't it!"

I decide I like Julia, very much. Although I go off her a bit when she lobs her bouquet right at me.

The next day is less of a cause for celebration. My family descends on me for lunch – mum, Big Brother, lovely wife, lovely kids, the lot. I like them too much to cook them a meal, so we adjourn to J's.

Everything's going fine until Reggie arrives. He's met my mum before, and the two of them chat while I catch up with my nieces' latest achievements in gymnastics, music and spying on their neighbours with a telescope. I'm absorbed in their exploits and almost leap from my seat when my mum exclaims, "You never told us you were going to be *published*! We didn't even know you'd finished the book!"

Before I can strangle Retired Reggie, champagne and glasses arrive. I drink deep, and decide explanations can wait. But eventually, I have to tell them.

"Spread WHAT?" chokes my mother.

"Spread betting," says Retired Reggie. "Derivatives. You trade the underlying market. Can go short, as well as long. No capital gains. Or brokerage fees. All tax free. Everyone's doing it. Friend of Sally's made ten million dollars in an afternoon."

I can't remember the last time my mother and I were simultaneously speechless. I recover first. "The novel's finished and I'm trying to get an agent." I try to sound upbeat, although I know how difficult it is to get decent representation. I've come across an outfit called agentresearch.com. Their job is to identify the agent who's right for me and my novel. I have a hit list of ten possibles, and I'm about to send begging letters to them all.

Meanwhile, there's this spread betting thing...

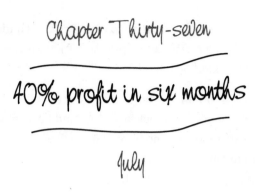

Chapter Thirty-seven

40% profit in six months

July

I return to the dealing room at Finspreads. This time, my mentor is an extremely fit trader called Jai. He pulls up my career trading record:

- 97 winning trades

- 84 losers

That's a better strike rate than my friend Mads, the pro hedge fund manager! But my joy is short-lived:

- I've won £6,439

- And lost £15,187

While I am still doing the maths – I discovered months ago that I am numerically dyslexic and frequently confuse 6's and 9's – Jai seeks to console me. "It's not as bad as you think." he says. "No-one wants to lose, but you've basically made the same mistake over and over again. You don't know when to close your bad trades. It's why we place such emphasis on stop-losses. They prevent you from getting into this kind of a mess."

I reflect guiltily on all the times that I've cancelled a stop-loss, convinced the market is about to recover and I can avoid losing a trade and losing money. And about all the times I've been wrong about this. I remind myself almost 50% of my losses accrued during May, when I was trading far too heavily, far too ignorantly, and far too stubbornly.

Things can only get better.

Jai shows me his own trading record. Finspreads staff aren't allowed to play the markets for real, but they're permitted to operate test accounts:

- He had begun with a bank of £5,000

- He'd grown it to £7,000

- 40% profit in six months

So what's Jai doing right? I study the print-out of his trades:

- He began by staking an average of £3 a point

- As he's become successful, he's increased this to £5 a point

- Most often, he day trades the FTSE and the Dow

- Jai's most successful trade is a profit of £400, backing the Dow to rise at £5 a point

- His biggest loser is £160 on a £5 a point Cable trade

- Losses are rarely more than £100 on any one trade

"How come so many of your trades close at break-even?" I ask.

Jai smiles. "That's a way to get a free bet," he explains. "Suppose I buy the FTSE at 5900 and it rises to 5930. I'm thirty points in profit, and I move the stop-loss up from – say – 5875 to 5900. So now, even if the FTSE does drop back, I can't lose."

I'm starting to get the message.

- I MUST use stop-losses

- I should stick to just a few markets and build my expertise

- I MUST use stop-losses

- I need to use moving averages

- I MUST use stop-losses

- And observe support and resistance levels

- I MUST use stop-losses

"One last thing." Jai sounds like Colombo. "Let me show you these." He pulls up a screen called Binary Bets. "You should have a try at these, some time."

But I'm no longer paying attention. I'm sure I just saw the Welshman walking along the corridor.

Chapter Thirty-eight

In which I have my head examined

One Week Later

I email the Welshman. "Was that you I saw today?"

A week later, he replies. "In Boston...very busy...new projects...must have lunch some time soon..."

I get another brush off. This time from the hot-shot literary agent Ed Victor. Bastard.

But not everyone is avoiding me. My publishers know I'm on the look out for a trading guru who's prepared to help me, and they've been in touch with another of their authors.

He's called John Piper, and his email to me has an attachment. It opens to reveal something headed Trading & Psychology Questionnaire. I am instructed to complete it before we go any further.

Blimey! One-hundred-and-fifty-five questions requiring my attention. In categories ranging from Motivation and Experience to

Results and Perception. It takes me an entire day to complete the questionnaire. Here are some edited highlights:

Q. **What's your primary reason for trading markets?**

A. A stubborn wish to learn how to get it right instead of watching real money disappear via a virtual trading screen.

Q. **Might the need for excitement have some part to play in the reason you trade markets?**

A. It's more exciting to win £500 on Google than spend an afternoon deciding where to put commas and semi-colons. It's definitely exciting when the markets are volatile and I'm trading the right way. But when it's going down like the water level in a leaky bucket? I'd rather play with my punctuation.

Q. **In monetary terms what are your goals in the market?**

A. Stop losing money. Start making money.

Q. **What's your worst trading experience?**

A. Berkeley. Gapped hugely overnight and I lost tons.

Q. **What do you think you learnt?**

A. Never to buy a Berkeley Home.

Q. **Do you use profit targets?**

A. I wish!

Q. **Would you prefer a 10% chance of making £10,000 or a 90% chance of making £1,000. Would it make any difference if the 90% chance was for £1,100, not just £1,000?**

A. Great question. Depends entirely on the circumstances. If it was a once-only opportunity (e.g. on a game show) I'd definitely go for the ten per cent chance of the higher sum…basically £1k isn't going to make much difference to me, but a lump sum of £10k would be cool. If, however, the 90% chance were recurrent then I'd prefer smaller, recurrent gains rather than the occasional jackpot. But this smells of 'trick question' to me. So let's do the maths:

- I place ten trades: Lose nine. Win one. End up with £10k

- I place ten trades. Win nine. Lose one. End up with £9k

- I place ten trades, Win nine. Lose one. End up with £9.9k

Verdict: I'd still find it emotionally more satisfying to be right nine out of ten. Then again, if you'd set the sums involved in hundreds of thousands, or millions, I think I could accommodate winning 'only' ten per cent of the time.

Q. **How do you feel after a string of five losses?**

A. Pissed off. But also knowing that if I continue to trade, rather than skulking off, I will inevitably secure a string of two wins, at least!

Q. **If the dartboard method works would you use it?**

A. You mean there's a dartboard method? Is this something to do with those double top chart patterns I'm supposed to look out for?

Q. **An orang-utan at San Diego zoo is calling the market with 86% accuracy. Do you follow the ape?**

A. Bloody right, I do. When can I meet this monkey?

Q. **If you had to liken the market to an animal, real, imaginary or otherwise, what animal would it be?**

A. Weasel.

Q. **Do you and your partner ever argue?**

A. Dow Jones definitely has a mind of his own.

Q. **Do you ever lie?**

A. Never ;)))

Q. **If everyone in a room had removed their shoes would you do the same?**

A. Yes, if it were someone's house and they were fastidious or neurotic about their furnishings. Or for a cultural reason. For exercise? Unlikely I'd even be in the room, but if I were, I'd most likely keep them on.

By the time I've completed the questionnaire, I am exhausted. But enlightened. I realise that when it comes to trading:

- I am not a trader at all – I am a gambler.

- I am foolish – relying on gut instinct and cursory research, rather than proper homework.

- I MUST use stop-losses from now on.

John Piper's book is couriered to me. It's called *The Way To Trade*. It makes sense. Every other trading book I've tried to read has been about, er, trading. Whereas here, the emphasis is on psychology – which means it's about me... what I'm doing... and how to improve what I do.

According to the blurb, John Piper lives in Dorking, Surrey, and in Massa, Italy.

Guess where I'm going to meet him?

Having negotiated the M25, I arrive in Surrey. It's a beautiful summer day and John opens his door wearing shorts. He has good legs. He looks a bit like Locke, the character in *Lost*.

Things get off to an inauspicious start when Dow Jones takes a dump on the immaculate lawn. John appears not to notice, and I clean up while he's making coffee.

Here's an interesting piece of trivia. Finspreads has more customers living in Dorking than anywhere else in the UK. John has coached some of them. "I often meet doctors and dentists who are looking for a new challenge," he tells me. "They want fun, and a bit of excitement, and trade a bit when they're bored."

But trading is no quick fix for boredom. "You need to have a methodology. Trade mechanically and leave all your emotions behind," John declares.

A methodology. Where could I get one of those? A writer friend of mine grew so exasperated when people asked where she got her plots from, she'd reply, "From Harrods, of course." I wonder if they sell methodologies, as well.

While I panic about methodology acquisition, John is telling me about his trading career. He's a former accountant, who:

- Made £20,000 in one month in his first year as a full-time trader

- Managed money for two years – and showed a profit five

months out of every six

- Made enough in one trade to buy a new Porsche

- Traded with over $1 million

- Got wiped out

- Made £10,000 in a single day trading futures

"Decide what you're going to do, and become an expert in it," he advises me. "Effectively, you need to make a trading business plan."

I drive home enlightened, but concerned. Where am I going to get a methodology?

Chapter Thirty-nine

I find my spread betting methodology tattooed on human flesh

August

Retired Reggie and Much Married Michael are devising their own money-making methodology. The only problem – it's illegal.

A couple of months ago, Camden increased the price of parking in Primrose Hill. Again. By our reckoning, the average parking ticket machine in Regents Park Road now earns roughly the same per annum as an apprentice hedge fund manager.

Reggie is outlining the concept. "The business model is this supermarket, not far from Macclesfield. It had twenty-one aisles with twenty-one tills. Only one problem." My friend pauses for dramatic effect. "There were only supposed to be twenty aisles and tills. The manager added an extra lane, and pocketed all the takings from the till that didn't officially exist."

"So all we have to do," Michael grins at the latest motorist who's emptying his wallet in exchange for a pay and display ticket, "is find out who sells these ticket machines, buy one, and set it up on the street for a few days."

I'm still in a blind panic about methodologies, so it's easier to shoot the breeze with my pals – although it's beginning to feel more like a chill wind of doom.

Reggie's internet fashion consultancy business is beginning to bear fruit. He's off to India next week. Michael's helping Julia to set up the Good Dog Training School – "Tossa's a miracle on four legs. You can't possibly fail," I encourage – and I'm in such acute need of a displacement activity that I've agreed to another internet blind date.

There's two guys who've been pursuing me. One, I know only as Scouse Git; he's a fan of my Finspreads blog, although he doesn't seem interested in spread betting, which is a bit weird. Still, his emails are peppered with one-liners, and they make me laugh. He's in the process of getting divorced, and it sounds rough. Or as he puts it: "Hell hath no fury like the lawyer of a woman scorned".

My other admirer is a paid-up member of the internet dating brigade. Goes by the online moniker of GeekWithSocialSkills, and looks a bit like Filthy Lucca, which is a plus. He's asked me out twice, but I've been 'busy'. Now I take the initiative, and arrange to meet him in a bar off Leicester Square.

GeekWithSocialSkills has overestimated the adjectival part of his name. He's definite eye candy, but conversation isn't one of his core skills. It's not that he can't string a sentence together. On the contrary. In the time it takes me to knock back a large vodka, I've been lectured about Web 2.0, social networking and folksonomic tagging. Whatever they are. I'm about to sneak off to the loo to call Supermum and ask her to pull the emergency text routine, when he gets to his feet.

"Another one, Sally," he offers, reaching for my empty glass. It seems mean to say no. And he is good looking. Maybe if I can get him to talk about earthly things…

When he comes back from the bar, GeekWithSocialSkills – actually, his name is Jason – removes his jacket.

"Eeug! What's *that*?" The words tumble from my mouth before I can edit them. I've always had a thing about tattoos. As in not liking them. And GeekWithSocialSkills – Jason – has a HUGE one. All the way up his naked right forearm. It's made up of 000's and 111's, in a random pattern. My immediate thought is that he had it done in prison.

"Oh, this!" GeekBoy swells with pride and runs a loving index finger over his own flesh. "My mum wasn't too keen on it either. But then I told her the story…"

Long before he's finished telling ME his Tattoo Tale, I'm wishing it was a bottle of vodka he'd bought me. I add ASCII control characters, octet code, caret notation and place-value notation to the list of words I never want to hear again.

But in the end, I get it.

If you're a lad who grew up friendless and closeted in a bedroom with only a computer for company, you'd just glance at GeekBoy's tattoo, give a post-ironic smile and tell him: "I don't think so!"

Because if you can read the language – and if you can, my money says you're also fluent in Klingon – the tattoo says: "I'm better than you."

It's written in binary code.

And I have stumbled upon my spread betting methodology.

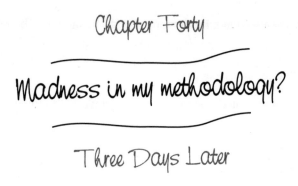

Chapter Forty

Madness in my methodology?

Three Days Later

Binary code. Binary bets. Remember? Jai at Finspreads had urged me to check out binaries. Now I could see exactly why he'd been enthusiastic about them.

Basically, a binary bet is a fixed odds bet, because you know your maximum gains and losses right away. But there are important differences:

- When you bet on England to beat Portugal, and Rooney gets sent off, you can prepare to kiss goodbye to your money, because once the game's begun, you can't change your bet.

- But with a financial fixed odds bet, you can bale out as soon as anything untoward happens, because prices are quoted – and changing all the time – until the market expires.

Here's an example of what I mean. You reckon the FTSE will close higher today than it did yesterday. By lunchtime, it's already up 32 points on the day, and the spread price is 74 – 80. Or as Jai had put it, when I called to ask him to explain binary bets in detail, "That means there's an 80 per cent chance that the FTSE will close higher."

- So I buy at 80 for £1 a point.

- The trade has only two possible outcomes (hence the name 'binary')

- If the FTSE finishes the day higher than yesterday's close, my bet settles at 100

- If the FTSE finishes lower than yesterday's close, my bet settles at zero

- Therefore, I'm either going to win £20 (the difference between 80 and 100)

- Or lose a maximum of £80 (the difference between 80 and zero)

- However…

- If the FTSE should weaken, I can close my trade early

- I'll lose, because I'll have to take the current sell price – which will definitely be falling

- For instance, if the sell price is down to 30 – I lose £50 (the difference between 80 and 30)

- But even if I do nothing except cross my fingers, the most I can lose is £80

You can also place hour-by-hour binary bets on the FTSE and the DOW. And there are binary markets for oil and currency, too.

I've spent two days riveted to the trading platform, watching the prices change to reflect the ups and downs of the FTSE and the Dow from opening time until the final bell.

Watching.

Learning.

And writing my methodology.

It goes like this...

Sally Nicoll's Binary Trading Methodology:

The Rationale

Successful binary trading seems to me to be micro management trading. To make it work, I need to be at my computer monitoring my trades, *all the time*. Although I can't use stop-losses, I'll know my maximum possible liability on any trade up front. And since every trade has a short, in-built deadline, I'll be unable to sit on losing positions for days on end. Having monitored the market and paper traded for a few days, I believe I can make money out of this! And as I said when I filled in the questionnaire I was given by John Piper – the Guru of Dorking – I'd prefer lots of little successes to the occasional jackpot.

The Methodology

Certain ground rules will be strictly observed:

- I will trade binaries on the following: FTSE and the DOW.

- I will trade what I SEE. Not what I think. No guesswork (as per John Piper's strict instructions!)

- I shall rely on technical analysis.

- I shall keep a record of every trade justifying my entry/exit decisions.

- Trades must have at least a 70% probability factor – and I will only enter at this level in circumstances where I am VERY confident.

- Generally speaking, I'll only enter trades with a probability factor of 85%.

- Only trades that have reached a 90%+ probability factor justify an investment of more than £1 a point.

- I will cut my losses when the market moves against me.

- I shall micro manage all open trades – if I am obliged to be away from my computer for more than two hours maximum (applies to a daily trade) I shall close the trade in order to preserve capital.

Money Management

John Piper has drummed into me that protecting my capital is the number one priority.

- BEST CASE – Make money

- WORST CASE – If I lose more than £500 in a week, I switch to Plan B: Can I bribe Mads to manage my Finspreads account alongside his hedge fund?

Tomorrow, it begins.

Chapter Forty-one

In which I turn my computer into a cash register

Mid-August

"Sally, are you OK? Have you gone away? We're all worried that the strain of trying to get some good spread betting results is proving, you know, a bit too much for you." The concern in Supermum's voice on my ansaphone is touching.

I've been neglecting my chums. Missed every morning meeting of the latterati in more than a week.

The truth is, I can't bear to tear myself away from the computer once the FTSE opens at 8 o'clock every morning.

I'm having too much fun.

Confession time. When I wrote down my methodology, I wasn't holding out much hope. John Piper's questionnaire had given me HUGE pause for thought. I realised I had developed the mentality of a loser. And that I needed to adjust my thinking.

My first session – Wednesday 9th August – started badly.

I overslept.

Things could only get better.

AND THEY DID!

Nothing in my inauspicious trading history had prepared me for the sheer thrill of the day. Watching the Japanese index climb in my favour back in January had been exciting. But nothing like this.

I couldn't stop placing winning trades.

I'd evidently chosen a good day to begin binary trading. The FTSE was heading upwards in an orderly direction. All I had to do was trade what I saw on the chart in front of me:

- The FTSE rose between 10am and 11am

- The FTSE rose between 11am and noon

- The FTSE rose between noon and 1pm

- The FTSE rose between 1pm and 2pm

- The FTSE rose between 2pm and 3pm

- The FTSE rose between 3pm and 4pm

- The FTSE ended the day 42 points higher

And I had winning trades.

Every single time.

I'm making it sound easy?

It was.

Every new mark on the chart had a meaning. The FTSE was going up. And down. Going down was good, because it meant I could get a better price if I wanted to buy.

Prices on the Finspreads platform change second by second with binaries. Here's a snapshot of the movements between 10am and 11am:

- 10.00: FTSE is already up 10 points from the previous hour – so the question is, will it be higher or lower in 60 minutes time?

- 10.01: Up 1.8 points – and the buy price is 70.6 (I think of this as 70% likely that FTSE will be higher at 11am than at 10am)

- 10.13: Down 1.1 points – buy price plummets to 48

- 10.18: Zero movement – buy price now 53

- 10.27: Up 0.3 points – buy price 51.9

- 10.31: Down 2.3 points – buy price 53.1

- 10.41: Up 1 point – buy price 78.3

- 10.52: Up 2.8 points – buy price 85.1

- 10.56: Up 2/6 points – buy price 100 (no more buy trades accepted)

(Prices shown relate to FTSE on 14 August 2006.)

The best time to buy in this example was at 10.13am. If you'd traded £2 a point, you'd have made £104 in forty-seven minutes. And £520 at £10 a point. Even the lawyers and plumbers I know don't earn that much.

But – as per my methodology – I keep my stakes low. To start with, at any rate. On Golden Wednesday, as I think of it, I feel as confident as I used to, all those years ago, when I played pinball in Portsmouth. Come to think of it, there are a few similarities: the score keeps changing… you need fast fingers to grab the best price… and I definitely feel in control, coming out of trades early, if I there seems any risk of an upset.

During the day I place thirteen trades. Most of my winnings are for modest amounts: £20.10, £11.40p, £1.60 (I had waited till the buy price was up all the way to 98.4 before risking my quid!), £13.20. These all come from hourly trades.

I'd also increased the size of my trades on the Up on the Day market, as the FTSE climbed. I bought for £1 a point when the price was 46 (breaching my own methodology already. But I swear I traded what I saw – and not through rose-tinted spectacles, either), another £2 a point at 64.8 and £3 a point at 65.3.

I groaned when the FTSE closed. But not for the usual reasons.

I had made £271.10 on the day.

Can I do it again on Wednesday?

I begin by making a big mistake. I'm too eager to get a punt on between 10 and 11. I buy early, and the price whiplashes. As per the methodology, I cut my trade, which costs me £66.80 at £2 a point. Could have been worse…

I don't lick my wounds. The hour is still young, and I want my money back. The first opportunity comes ten minutes later: the price is going back up, and now I think I was premature in getting out of that trade. I buy another £2 a point at a price of 89.8. With a few minutes to go, the price is up to 90.9. I do some quick stuff with my calculator and buy for £6 a point.

For once, my maths is correct:

- Trade One: -£66.80

- Trade Two: £20.40

- Trade Three: £54.60

- Overall: I win £8.20

OK, so £8.20 won't even buy you a morning's parking in Primrose Hill. (Just as well, as they'll probably tow you away after two hours.) But that's not the point. For the first time in my spread betting career, I've *traded*. As opposed to gambled. Initially, I'd protected my capital, when it seemed the trade was a bad one. Then I re-entered the market because of what the chart was telling me. And finally, I worked out how much I needed to trade per point, in order to get into profit.

Well done me. On Day Two of Trading With Methodology, I place 14 trades for a net profit of £34.10. My winnings are more modest, mostly because I'm growing cautious – as much as I like Finspreads, I don't want to give them back the previous day's winnings.

Day Three isn't so hot. Today, the FTSE falls, and it takes me longer than it should to get my head around the fact that I need to sell rather than buy. Once I've readjusted my thinking, I make five successive winning trades for a total of £141.19. Not bad, but too little, too late. At least I mop up the earlier losses I've accrued. Eleven trades in total and I've lost £49.80 on the day. Which, incidentally, is a Friday. I blame Mads and his hedge fund chums for closing their positions so they can enjoy the weekend. Next time, I'll remember to be more cautious about buying on a Friday.

Next morning, I am desolate. The markets are closed. I begin to understand why binary betting has been described as the crack cocaine of spread betting. There's the weekend, I catch up with my neglected pals.

One guess what we talk about.

It's scorching hot so we take Tossa and Dow Jones to the Hill, to scare the tourists. My dog immediately charms three groups of al fresco diners into feeding him sausages, prawns and chicken breast, but then things take an embarrassing turn for the worse. Dow-Wow chases Tossa into the bushes where he – let me put this delicately – is first to realise she's on heat, and relieves her of her virginity. Dow Jones is promptly enrolled into the Good Dog Accelerated Training Program, if only to appease Much Married Michael.

I'm relieved when Monday comes, and I can get back to my trading screen. The FTSE's meandering around, so there are few good opportunities. By lunchtime I've made enough for a dog training session. So in the afternoon, I turn my attention to the Dow.

This is so easy!

The market is up over 90 points within two hours – and it's obviously going to be one of those days where the buy price on the daily Dow will be at 100 even before it's lunchtime in New York.

Fortunately, I've got my trades on early: £7 at a price from 83.2 to 92.2.

Eassssssssy.

My first inkling that even when the price is shown as 100, I'm not home and dry, comes while I am totting up my projected winnings. WHAT'S GOING ON? The Dow's tumbling far more rapidly than it climbed.

Now with only 30 minutes to go, it ventures into negative territory. I work out how much I'm going to lose. Over £600. This is horrible. I cut £3 from my position for a loss of £179.10 – with £7 still in play and looking very risky.

My television's tuned to Bloomberg. I can hear George Bush in the background, talking his usual bollocks.

But look! The Dow's responding. It's levitating like Lazarus. Going up with every sentence.

What do I do?

- I abandon the money management rules of my methodology

- I trade what I see

- I buy £2 a point at 80

- Another £10 a point at 84.8 (if I'm wrong, I'll lose £858 on this trade alone. But I know I'm not wrong – I'm trading what I see)

- With seconds to go, I add another £5 to my position at a price of 96.4

- Moments later, the Dow closes

- It's up on the day by 8.8 points

- My £10 trade makes me £152 (in the space of five minutes)

- The final reckoning: I'm £88 up on the day

- And shaking like a rabbit in Tossa's jaws

My four sessions of binary trading result in a net profit of £417.90. John Piper's going to be amazed.

What a triumphant way to end my Diary.

Finally, I am a winner.

But before I can write THE END and claim my advance from the publisher, something else happens.

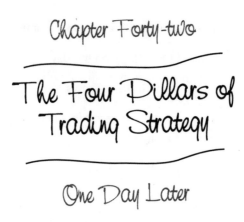

Chapter Forty-two

The Four Pillars of Trading Strategy

One Day Later

Retired Reggie is to blame.

There I am, enjoying the sunshine and a frappuccino, when he comes bustling along the street. "Sally, take a look at this!" And he thrusts a computer print-out into my hands. I half expect it to be an easyJet e-ticket, as I know Reggie is keen to meet the cousins he's discovered through Ancestry.com. One of them, Gerik, is also in the rag trade and together, they're plotting to dress the women of Warsaw in outfits based on this season's Topshop designs.

However, I find myself holding an invitation to a free seminar. It's called *Trading Secrets 2006* and according to the blurb, this is my opportunity to learn direct from a full-time professional trader called Greg Secker.

"I thought you might be able to use it for your Diary," says Reggie. "Get some hints and tips. That sort of stuff."

I take another look at the print-out. Here's what it promises to deliver:

- How to enter high-probability trades without getting stopped out – and having your trade cancelled

- How to know exactly which active sectors to be trading now for excellent results

- How to trade with only 1% risk for huge upside potential

- Trade entry: how to get it right and bank the profits

- When to sell and take your large profit while you still have it

- Proven methods to maximise results and minimise losses

- How to identify chart patterns that indicate enormous stock moves – both up and down

Seductive stuff.

"Yeah, right," I roll my eyes. "It's going to be like one of those property seminars. Or a Moonie brainwashing job. You go along and get locked in a room for hours, until you sign on the dotted line for whatever it is they're selling."

Retired Reggie looks hurt. I know he was only trying to help. "Tell you what," I say. "I'll go along and find out what the scam is. You're right. I might be able to use it. "

Back home, I go online to book my place at the seminar. I take the name of one of my dearest friends in vain and give a false address to make sure the Secker organisation won't be able to pester me with junk mail forever after.

Then I check my emails. Good, another one from Scouse Git. I really look forward to his messages. They always make me laugh. He's pretty cagey about himself, but I've been asking questions and so far I have learned:

1 He's Liverpool born and bred

2 His first name is James – "But nobody ever calls me that"

3 Works every once in a while

4 Has a house in North London

5 Been married twice and has four kids

6 Is older than me

7 Knows how to play a guitar

8 Hasn't tried spread betting yet – but might do, one day

9 Is left-handed

10 Owns a Wheaten terrier

It couldn't be? Could it? Oh, if only…

I spend thirty minutes Googling "Paul McCartney". Then I tell myself to get a life.

It's strange not having any work to do. I'm steering clear of binary trading, just in case I screw up, lose my profits and feel morally obliged to report the fact. But in the long run, I'm already convinced it's the way forward for me as a trader.

I take Dow-Wow to the park, and we bump into Much Married Michael, Julia and Tossa. Soon, we are all back at J's, discussing

Camden Council's latest money-making atrocities. Apparently, there's a camera on Haverstock Hill that's earning £1,500 a day by spying on motorists who stray into the badly-marked bus lane, and then issuing them with fines.

"That's over half a million in a year!" Michael's calculation is so fast, I wonder why he doesn't take up spread betting. But the Good Dog Training School is doing well – locals are now obliged to get their puppies' names on the waiting list at birth, if not sooner – and the way Julia looks at Michael, you get the impression that if he ever does go back to Venice, it will be with her.

It feels as though summer is nearly over, and we are all moving on with our lives. What's next for me? Literary agents aren't exactly beating a path to my door; perhaps it's time to acknowledge that my sabbatical is over, and I need to resurrect my advertising career. My mum will be relieved, although the prospect doesn't exactly fill me with joy.

The next day, I arrive at one of those anonymous yet prosperous Kensington hotels, in good time for Greg Secker's seminar.

The registration desk is manned by a beaming Australian greeter, armed with an eager smile and a clipboard. "And you are?" he asks.

"Sal…Marianne Haunfelder."

"Great to meet you Salmarianne!" Direct eye contact and a bone-crunchingly firm handshake. "Nice name. Is it Spanish?"

"Er, no." I flee inside the room, wiggling my fingers to see if they've been broken.

"You're very lucky, today," the Australian accent follows me through the swing door. "Greg himself is here!"

I smile grimly to myself. This is exactly what I expected. They're trying to make me feel as if I'm in the presence of God the Trader, all the better to part me from my money.

There are about thirty of us in the seminar room. Mostly blokes. On the seats are various handouts. I single out the one that's printed on Financial Times pink. "Here's what people are saying about Traders University," it says. Ah, so that's what they're selling…

I turn to the testimonials.

> "I started as an absolute beginner… one month later, I made £9,328 – tax free – while I was presenting a lecture," says a bloke with a PhD.

> "…over £400 profit from a short on Lonmin while I was at work," gloats another.

I'm wondering sanctimoniously if their employers are aware of this electronic moonlighting when the lights in the room go dim and a video kicks in. A man begins to speak. Greg Secker, I presume. Despite the fact that I am here to jeer, I can't help but notice that he's undeniably cute. The video voiceover is much as you would expect: "…people are unwilling to invest in themselves… not down to luck… strategy not emotion…'" and just as my lip curls at the live-the-dream montage of Mediterranean mansions, sunsets and speedboats, we're all plunged back into daylight. Greg Himself enters from the back of the room and walks smilingly to the stage.

"I've taught over 7,000 people to trade," he informs us. "But before I tell you more, let's go back to May. When the markets plunged, remember? Was that painful, or did you have fun?" Greg scrutinises the audience and I shift uneasily in my chair, thinking about all the money I'd squandered, because I'd been too stubborn to cut my losses.

"We had a lot of fun," Greg continues. He takes us through the testimonials, telling us a little about his students. "This one, he's now consistently making around £2,500 a week – he used to be a professional footballer."

Ah! Here's my chance to discover if any of these claims are true. I whip out my phone, connect to Google and type in the bloke's name. Sure enough – he played for Portsmouth, Reading and Sheffield United.

Just as I begin to readjust my thinking, Greg says, "I'm hoping you'll want to come on the course I run. It costs around £3,000. For which you get two intensive days of training, ongoing professional coaching for six months and lots of other good things. And now I've got that out of the way, let's talk about trading."

This catches me unaware. I'd been expecting two hours of big fluffy promises, followed by a sales pitch that went on-and-on-and-on while being vague about the cost.

"My big thing is risk," Greg continues. "In fact, trading is a code word for risk. When it's good it's really exciting, but too many people play the game without knowing what the hell is going on."

I sense a mood of empathy rippling through the room.

"How much do you guys lose on an average trade?" Greg asks.

Uneasy shuffling. No-one is eager to speak.

"Your losses should all have something in common," he tells us. "They should never amount to more than one per cent of your trading bank. Unless you get that right, a few losing trades will hit you like a freight train, and then it's all over."

In the audience, we're all beginning to exchange bashful smiles.

"How much should you put on a spread bet? Hands up everyone who consistently plays for the same stake per point?"

A few hands go up. Smiles become more assured. At least some of us are getting something right some of the time.

Apparently not. Greg explains money management techniques. If your maximum acceptable loss is £100, and your stop-loss needs to be 20 points away, then you can afford to spread bet at £5-a-point. Everybody gets it, and for most of us, it's a revelation.

"Now I'm going to show you the difference between punting and trading," he says.

I find myself liking Greg Himself Secker. Soon, along with the rest of the audience, I am scribbling notes as fast as he can speak. Which is almost as fast as the aforementioned freight train.

- I learn how I could have made £1,464 profit from Royal Dutch Shell in ten days, while putting only £168 of my £17,000 trading bank at risk.

- I draw diagrams of trading cycles – they look a bit like an outline of Bart Simpson's head, but already I can see what I've been doing wrong.

- I learn the importance of undersized bars on a chart – they mean a market is becoming less volatile and consolidating, which is often the prelude to trading nirvana: a lucrative breakout that you've anticipated right from the off.

Greg had promised us refreshments, but we beg him not to stop. Everyone's entranced, as though we're listening to the Sermon on the Mount or the result of the X Factor.

The two hours fly past, and the ride is more Concorde than freight train. It's a Master Class in trading. And it ends with Greg's Four Pillars of Trading Strategy:

1   Select growth-oriented, hot sectors

2   Then select the performing stocks in the sectors

3   Use combined signals – moving averages are important – to know when to open your trade

4   Remember to lock in profits by moving the stop-loss upwards as your trade gains in value, and use the signals again to decide when to close your trade

The session draws to a close.

Even though it means confessing my name is not Salmarianne, I join the queue of people who are signing up for Greg Secker's course.

Chapter Forty-three

I attend Traders University

Monday

Dow Jones is taking his GCSEs – that's General Canine Safety Evaluation – at the Good Dog Training School. It's a big day for me, too: I'm off to Traders University.

Since my book deadline is now imminent, Greg Secker has arranged for me to join the fast track: I'm to spend a very long day going one-on-one with a trading coach called Xavier.

"So you're Sally," he greets me. "I've read your stuff on Finspreads, and it made me laugh. But for all the wrong reasons."

Xavier is mean. There's no offer of coffee. No cosy getting-to-know you chat. Before I can say, "Two sugars and plenty of milk, please," I am in front of a computer and my training has begun.

In a class of one, there is nowhere to hide. We begin to analyse charts, and soon I am being asked to identify ascending triangles... descending triangles... bull flags... bear pennants. After several false starts, I begin to make progress, and bask in Xavier's smile of approval.

I learn that from now on, I will be ignoring newspapers, brokers and tipsters. I will never need to waste money on promise-the-earth trading systems. As of now, only one thing really matters: *Price action*.

"Price action is at the heart of the Traders University methodology, which you *must* follow for all of your trades," Xavier declares.

Before lunchtime I have gained a whole new circle of Dearest Friends. 350 of them – the stocks that make up the FTSE 350 Index. Soon, I will be as familiar with their names as I am with my own.

"You'll be analysing the whole lot," Xavier tells me cheerfully.

And by the time you've filtered them correctly, you'll be left with just a handful of red-hot stocks to follow." He clicks to a different screen on the computer. "Like these," he says.

I look at Xavier's two trades of the day: BT and British Land. He's nicely ahead on both. It's hard to argue. And anyway, we have work to do.

The Traders University syllabus is focused on momentum trading, which means trying to profit from trades that usually last from five to fourteen days.

Topics covered include: economic indicators… why I should focus only on certain sectors at particular times… finding the chart patterns that leap from the screen and shout: *"Buy me!"* … areas of indecision… continuation patterns… wedge formations… reversal patterns…

It's hard not to envy Dow Jones. All he has to do is balance biscuits on his nose, weave in and out of a few poles, sit and stay, and retrieve a few balls.

"You're doing great, Sally." Xavier hands me a sandwich along with his words of encouragement. "We'll make a trader of you yet."

By the time the sun goes down, I am beginning to master the Traders University methodology. My head's hurting, but I really am getting the hang of it.

You filter, filter, filter:

- Many of the FTSE 350 get dumped right away (like guys who go clubbing dressed in sports jackets).

- Others survive the preliminary cut but lose out once you get to know them a bit better (like guys whose kisses remind you of a Dyson).

- Until eventually, you find The One (which makes me think of Scouse Git).

And by the time I've drawn up my hit list of potential trades, fixed my entry points, calculated the profit potential and done the money management bit, I've decided Xavier isn't so bad, after all. In fact, he's a damn good teacher.

Greg Himself joins us. He's installed ShareScope Pro trading software on my computer, so I can analyse the markets. It costs about £80 a month – for which you get real-time, moment-by-moment prices, indicators, a news feed and all sorts of goodies – and with my new-found knowledge and methodology, I anticipate it will more than pay for itself.

Xavier tells Greg I've been a good student, and we fix a time for my first coaching session.

It sounds as though my day has finally ended. But no, there's more. Greg isn't going home just yet. "Come and have a look at this," he invites.

I follow him to another computer. Greg's own face stares out of it in high definition. I swivel my head back to the real thing. It's kind of spooky. I'm looking at something called Live Trading Floor.

"Basically, it does what it says on the tin," says Greg. "You can sit at home and look over my shoulder, and see the trades we're making, hour by hour, day by day, as we open and close them."

"Are you winning?"

"Oh, yes! Here, take a look."

More clicks, and I'm looking at Greg's list of recent trades. Plenty of losers. But the gains definitely outweigh the duds:

Winners:

- £1,520 Shire – buy

- £552 Intercontinental Hotels – sell

- £810 Gyrus – buy

Losers:

- £62.50 Tesco – buy

- £82.50 Corus Group – buy

- £72 Petrofac – buy

"Now look at this!" Greg's enthusiasm is infectious. He reminds me of a kid opening his Christmas presents. Nonetheless, I'm impressed. Live Trading Floor is cutting-edge stuff. There's a video clip for every trade, showing exactly why it was placed.

Now I'm the one who's entranced. I watch. I learn. Greg gets me out of the office only once I've signed up for Live Trading Floor.

I grab a cab back to Primrose Hill to collect Dow Jones from Much Married Michael and Julia. My dog is sporting a bright blue rosette, munching on a pig's ear – his favourite snack – and looking very pleased with himself.

Hardly surprising. He's aced his GCSEs: A* for agility, obedience and retrieval, although only a C for the biscuit balancing. "We'll have to work on that, won't we?" Julia hands me a clutch of certificates and gives Dow-Wow a fond pat.

Home at last. Before I turn in for the night, I check my emails.

Three literary agents want to read my novel. Two in London and one in New York. And Scouse Git says he wouldn't mind meeting me some time.

I'm more excited about the literary agents.

But it's a tough call.

Chapter Forty-four

I break the Traders University rules – and the promise of imminent wealth is dangled before me

The Next Day

There was a friend of a friend at the London Business School who was apparently accused of cheating on his course in Ethics. Which posed the dilemma: should he be expelled for his morally reprehensible behaviour, or rewarded with an A* for initiative?

I never did find out what happened, but I remember the incident as I sit and wrestle with my own conscience. This is the thing: the deadline for getting my Diary to the publisher is just five days away. I'm desperate to end with a winning streak that tops even my binary trading achievements. And I think I know how to do it.

I can cheat.

What if I simply log onto Live Trading Floor, look over the shoulder of Greg Himself and copy his trades? Aren't I bound to get a few winners?

But then again, what's the point? Where's the glory if you cheat your way to victory? I thrust temptation aside and spend the afternoon scouring ShareScope for red-hot trades.

Ah ha! Here's one! Pendragon. For the next forty minutes I stalk it as if I were Dow-Wow on the scent of a squirrel. I calculate my entry point, my exit, my stop-loss and my potential profit.

Finally, I make my move.

I short Pendragon. At £15 a point.

The share price duly falls and I start making money within a couple of hours, which I interpret as a reward from the gods for choosing the path of righteousness.

The following day, Xavier and I get together for our first coaching session. There's no need for me to go back to the Traders University HQ. Instead, we hook up by way of some very cool technology: a combination of Skype and video conferencing software that lets us to talk to one another while looking at my trading screens.

"My short on Pendragon. It's ahead." I'm excited and proud.

"Let me have a look."

The chart appears simultaneously on my screen in Primrose Hill and his in Fulham.

"Hmm." An ominous response fills the air in North London. "Why are you trading Pendragon?" Xavier asks.

"Because it's falling."

"I can see that. But that's not what I mean."

"Look. I went in for £15-a-point at 514.1. And I'm in profit." Which part of profit does Xavier not understand?

"But look at the moving averages, Sally."

I look.

"They're not where they're supposed to be. Are they?"

Er, no. But I'm in profit. Up £96.

"That's the whole point of the methodology you've learned. To screen stocks in a very specific way. And this trade breaks the rules. Doesn't it?"

Sulkily, I acknowledge that it does.

"I can see why you chose it," Xavier softens. "It's almost a fit, but not quite." I hear him sighing across the Skype as I explain my other picks. The trades I'm planning to place once my coach has congratulated me for being such a fast learner.

But he's not impressed. "What did we say about the daily close? And where does the next bar on the chart have to be?"

I feel like a child being told off by its parent. The fact that Xavier is correct doesn't help.

I promise in future to trade by the rules, and we fix our next interrogation. Coaching session, I mean.

My ego needs stroking. And it's about to be fondled. One of London's most influential literary agents wants to meet me. His client list reads like a Who's Who of famous authors.

I scoot over to his office, before he has a chance to change his mind. It's just as I imagined – everywhere you look are books, books and more books. I'm tempted to ask for free samples.

"Your novel," says Famous Literary Agent. "We like it. A lot."

Before I know what's happening, there's a glass of champagne in my hands. It's not even lunchtime. This is the life!

At least it seems so until Famous Literary Agent suggests, "There's just one little problem in the storyline concerning the Queen. The cancer scenario. Bit of a turnoff. Could she perhaps have a riding accident?"

I promise to think about it.

And as if afraid I might not be sufficiently impressed with the representation on offer, Famous Literary Agent moves in for the kill. "About twice a year," he tells me, "someone sits where you're sitting right now. And six weeks later, they're incredibly rich. No promises, but we might be able to do that for you."

On the strength of this, I abandon the Northern Line in favour of a black cab. We're halfway down Albany Street when my mobile rings.

"Sally!" My Big Brother is breathless with excitement. "Have you seen this week's *Investors Chronicle*? That guru of yours. Greg Secker. They say he's a charlatan."

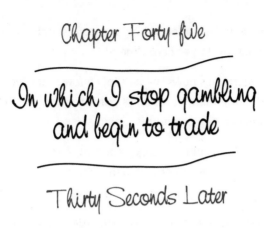

Chapter Forty-five

In which I stop gambling and begin to trade

Thirty Seconds Later

The cab driver screeches to a halt at the next newsagents. I leap out and buy *Investors Chronicle*. They've devoted five pages to Greg Secker. Kebabed him, as my media pals would say. I read the article with mounting bewilderment.

According to the article, Greg claims at his free seminars that he can "teach people to turn £2,000 or £3,000 into £10,000 without risk."

He said nothing of the sort at the one I went to. On the contrary. Greg's big on risk – and how to minimise it. He preaches the Gospel of Stop-Loss in a major way and the money management elements of the Traders University syllabus make it crystal clear that trading is a risky business.

I read on. The basic thrust of the article is that Greg promises the earth but can't possibly deliver. That he's laughing all the way to the bank by promising students they can consistently increase their trading capital by 15 per cent a month.

Again, this comes as news to me. Only a few hours earlier, Xavier had been telling me that trading's hard work – and that like any other skill it has to be learned.

Back to the article. I turn the page expecting to read about angry ex-students who've been wiped out in the markets. Curiously enough, there are none.

Instead, there's someone who apparently attended Traders University and made £23,000 over five months from capital of £250,000 – in other words, a 9 per cent return.

Sounds pretty good to me.

I read on. "Traders University suggests to students that losses are a sign you need more coaching."

What's so terrible about this? For me, the ongoing coaching offered by Traders University is part of its appeal.

Have I been brainwashed?

Is Greg Secker a Moonie in disguise?

Indignant on his behalf, I spend the Bank Holiday Monday screening the entire FTSE 350.

Filter, filter, filter.

There's more at stake than just Greg's reputation. I have precisely two trading days in which to accomplish something useful. On Thursday, I fly to New York to meet the other literary agents who are romancing me. My publishers are asking awkward questions – "Where's our manuscript?" – so this is my final chance to prove myself.

Filter, filter, filter.

I have selected 51 potential longs and 12 potential shorts.

"What did we say about moving averages?" I no longer need Skype – Xavier's instructions are playing in my head.

Filter, filter, filter.

You know what? I'm really enjoying this! Once you know what you're doing, it's like studying the form before you place your bets at the race course.

I know what I'm looking for: trades that have the potential to make me money.

Filter, filter, filter.

The market's positive, so I'm going to focus on buying rather than selling.

Which means I'm taking some of my profit on Pendragon right away. £97.50 is added to my Finspreads account. Xavier will be pleased I'm out of the trade. I reckon I've made an auspicious start.

Remember the excitement of binary trading?

This is nothing like that.

Instead, I feel like a General going into battle. Commanding my troops. Executing my game plan. I feel calm and in control. Even if it all goes horribly wrong, I know how – and when – to retreat.

- My top priority is to preserve my capital.

- Every trade I place will be protected with a stop-loss.

- My greatest weakness is that because I've put myself under pressure to produce quick results, I may be tempted to overtrade.

- I have a manuscript to finish, a suitcase to pack, and at least a dozen errands to run, so I shan't be sitting at my computer all day, watching share prices. I must place my trades and then get on with my life.

Happily, the Finspreads trading platform now allows me to place opening stop orders. This has nothing to do with getting in early at the pub. It means that if and when the price hits the level I've specified, my trade is automatically triggered.

By the time the markets close, I've decided what clothes I'm taking to New York, sorted out travel insurance, apologised to Dow Jones for sending him to stay with Much Married Michael, Julia and Tossa for a few days, and booked a hotel just off Times Square.

And my trades? The results for Day One are as follows:

- Pendragon – WIN £97.50

- Gyrus – LOSE £36.50

- Johnson Matthey – WIN £77.50

- AstraZeneca – LOSE £20.50

- Aviva – LOSE £27.69

- United Utilities – WIN £50.51

So I've won three, lost three, and made a net profit of £140.82 on the day.

I'm tempted to report my results to *Investors Chronicle*, but instead I get back to ShareScope and prepare for my final trading session.

Filter, filter, filter.

I'm particularly pleased with my losing trade on AstraZeneca. I slightly misjudged my entry point, hence the loss, but the share price reached a four-year-high today – at 3374 – and I'm optimistic the trend will continue tomorrow. I have £4-a-point that says it will.

Filter, filter, filter.

My trades are in place for Wednesday. I'm seriously excited about going to New York. And I've got a date with Scouse Git fixed for when I get back.

Now all I need is for the markets to move my way.

Ready for the final results?

Here they are:

- Forth Ports – LOSE £57.20

- Johnson Matthey – WIN £52.50

- Lloyds – WIN £2

- Royal Bank of Scotland – WIN £17.50

- AstraZeneca – WIN £112

- Aviva – WIN £35

- United Utilities – WIN £60

- Cairn Energy – WIN £40

That's seven wins out of eight (Forth Ports had been a short and it didn't quite meet the Traders University criteria, but let's not tell Xavier) for a net profit of £261.18.

So now I have an extra £402.62 to spend in New York!

Am I leaping up and down in excitement? Dancing with delight now that my Diary has its Happy Ending?

Er, no.

I'm quietly contemplating…

Contemplating the fact I've finally discovered what profitable spread betting is all about:

It's not about gambling.

It's not about investing.

It's about trading.

Chapter Forty-six

Sex, lies and Paul McCartney

September

I persuaded the publishers to extend my deadline so I could bring you the rest of the story.

I could have flown back from New York without needing a plane. I've landed the literary agent of my very best dreams – the guy who helped make Robert Ludlum famous. Let's hope he can do the same for me, and if he can't, then at least he'll feel obliged to wangle me an invitation to meet Matt Damon next time he plays Jason Bourne, the character Robert Ludlum created.

I just got off the phone with Greg Secker. He's decided not to sue for defamation. "The lawyer told me I had a clear case for defamation. He also said that if I pursued a claim, I'd be helping put his two kids through school and university. Strangely enough, the article's had a great effect on my business – people are turning up to the seminars because they read about me in *Investors Chronicle*!"

I've also found time for a coffee with an old colleague of mine, Beirut Bob. "Sally, I'm going to make a fortune!" he greets me. "I'm taking up trading. I've come across this amazing system. A software package that tells you when to get into trades and when to get out. It's amazing. Only costs £4,000. What have you been up to?"

I tell him what I've been doing lately. I add that there are no short cuts in trading. That software systems don't work – if they did, everyone would use them, everyone would place exactly the same trades and the market would cease to function, because it requires buyers *and* sellers. I suggest that Bob should consider reading a few books, joining the Finspreads Academy and trading at a penny a point. He doesn't like what he's hearing, and changes the subject. I'm left wondering why Greg Secker found himself in the financial dock when there are so many real conmen out there selling impossible dreams.

I also bumped into Sandy Jadeja. "Sally, I'm so sorry I couldn't squeeze you onto my course," he sounds truly repentant. "It really was down to health and safety regulations. I'm changing hotels for the next one."

John Piper? Believe it or not, he's taken up binary trading and is convinced he's going to make a fortune. Now that *is* interesting, and provided Finspreads don't sack me when they read this Diary, I'll keep you posted on his progress.

There's just one final thing to write about.

My date with Scouse Git.

He'd invited me to dinner at The Wolseley. It's a beautiful place – all vaulted high ceilings, crisp linen napery, beautiful chandeliers and grand marble pillars – a mecca for A list celebs and it definitely beats the hell out of Starbucks in Golders Green.

"I still don't know what you look like," I email him.

"Don't worry," comes the reply. "You'll know me when you see me. We need to be discreet. All will become clear."

Would you tell your dearest friends that you're going on a date with Paul McCartney? Neither do I. The only person I'm tempted to confide in is my mum, but I'm frightened she'll say Macca's much too old for me, and insist on going in my place.

I spend three hours getting ready and change my outfit six times.

By the time I arrive at The Wolseley, I'm shaking. Last time I was this nervous, the price of gold was sinking by the second – and I'd predicted exactly the opposite.

They're expecting me.

"Miss Nicoll. Very pleased you can be with us this evening," beams the Maître d'. "This way."

He guides me through the web of tables to what looks like a more private area at the back.

And I see him before he sees me.

Paul McCartney.

Live and in the flesh.

But who's that woman he's with?

Dear God. Not another bloke who brings his ex on a date? She's wearing a suit. Maybe it's his lawyer. Will I have to sign a pre-nup before I get any soup?

"This way, Miss Nicoll." The Maître d' gently brushes my shoulder. What's going on? Why am I being guided past Paul McCartney's table – shouldn't someone be pulling out a chair for me?

And then I see them.

Retired Reggie.

Much Married Michael.

Julia.

Don the Drug Dealer.

Supermum.

My mum.

Big Brother.

They've even located the Welshman.

All sitting at one table.

And I'm the guest of honour.

After I have finished swearing at Retired Reggie for pretending to be Paul McCartney – I never should have encouraged the old rogue to become computer literate – I ask him, "But how did you know Macca would be here tonight?"

"A happy accident. Shall we go and get his autograph?"

The evening turns into the best date I've had all year.

And there my story ends.

Almost.

My new literary agent says every good book needs a healthy dash of sex. Even this one. Fortunately, I'd anticipated his recommendation by way of the steamy scene a few chapters back.

What do you mean, you missed it?

You remember…Dow-Wow and Tossa. In the bushes. Back in the summer on Primrose Hill.

Six extremely curious-looking puppies were born last week. Mother and Father are doing well.

The End

And finally… £50 from Finspreads*

So have I put you off spread betting?

I hope not.

After all, I've made every mistake in the book, so that you don't have to.

I feel my real trading career is only just beginning. Now I've got a taste for what's really involved, I'm eager to get better.

I hope you'll follow my progress by clicking on my Diary on the Finspreads web site at www.finspreads.com.

And do come and visit my own web site: www.sallynicoll.com.

If you think you can do better at spread betting than me, then here's your chance to try it for yourself.

The nice people at Finspreads are making a special offer for my readers. I think it's pretty hot:

• You'll be enrolled in the Finspreads Academy

• You can trade for just 1p a point to begin with

• And your new account – you can open it with a minimum of £100 – will be topped up with a bonus of £50

You'll find full details on www.finspreads.com/sallynicoll

Good luck. I'd love to hear how you're getting on – email me at sally@sallynicoll.com

Sally Nicoll, Primrose Hill, October 2006

*Finspreads is a trading name of IFX Markets Ltd. Sally Nicoll is an appointed representative IFX Markets Ltd which is authorised and regulated by the Financial Services Authority. Spread betting carries a high level of risk to your capital with the possibility of losing more than your initial investment and may not be suitable for all investors. Ensure you fully understand the risks involved and seek independent advice if necessary.

APPENDIX

John Piper's Trading and Psychology Questionnaire

(Extracted from *The Way to Trade*, Harriman House Publishing)

This questionnaire is extensive in its scope. The more fully you answer the various questions the more useful will be the feedback I can give you. However this is not intended to be an interrogation and if you do not wish to answer any question please just state by the side of that question "No answer provided ". Some answers require more than just a single word, in these cases feel free to use a separate sheet, but please reference each such answer to the question to which it relates.

The questions are deliberately not standardised, so you are free to answer (or not) as you see fit.

The questionnaire is designed to give you insights into your trading and as such, it may pay you to spend some time in completing it. It should prove time well spent. Don't rush it!

If you would like feedback on your answers, send them to: John@ttttt.freeserve.co.uk

Trading

A. Motivation

1. What do you want from the markets?

2. How are you going to get it?

3. What will you then have? Describe your expected emotions.

4. What will you then want?

5. How are you going to get it?

6. What will you then have? Describe your expected emotions.

7. Repeat questions 4 – 6 in sequence until you reach a final answer.

8. What do you see as your primary reason for trading markets?

9. Do you have any secondary reasons?

10. Might the need for additional challenges have some part to play in the reason you trade markets?

11. Might boredom and the need to relieve it have some part to play in the reason you trade markets?

12. Might the need for excitement have some part to play in the reason you trade markets?

13. Might ego stimulation have some part to play in the reason you trade markets?

14. Might self esteem have some part to play in the reason you trade markets?

15. Is it possible that some or other of these emotions trigger you into trades at some points?

16. What do you see as other reasons that you take trades you ought not to take?

17. Which trading vehicles do you prefer? [Stocks/options/futures/CFD/spread betting]

18. Do you ever find yourself being unable to take trades?

19. What do you feel may be the reasons for this?

20. In monetary terms what are your goals in the market?

21. Do you see these as realistic?

22. Would you be able to achieve these goals whilst staying "cool, calm and collected"?

23. In view of your answers to questions 21 and 22, do you want to modify your reply to question 20?

B. Experience

1. Most traders wipe out before they learn the all important lesson to limit losses. Have you been through this experience? [Yes/No]

2. Please give details (write on a separate sheet if need be).

3. Describe the emotions associated with this event.

4. What do you think you learnt?

5. Do you feel that you have dealt with this experience fully?

6. Describe the fears that you now encounter trading markets?

7. List the trading actions you will not take. For example, not holding overnight, not trading futures or writing options etc.

8. Do you see these as limitations?

9. What sort of stops do you like to use?

10. Do you use specific methodologies?

11. Do you have only one or more then one? Give number.

12. Does this methodology give you precise entry/exit signals?

13. If not, why not?

14. Do you think the reasons given under 13 above are a positive or a negative to your trading success?

15. As a result of your answer to 14 above do you intend to take any action?

16. Why not?

17. Do you think that if your methodology was more precise that you would learn more about why you sometimes take inappropriate trading signals?

18. Do you think inappropriate means anything to do with resultant profits or losses?

19. If so, why?

20. Do you use profit targets?

21. If so, why?

22. Do you have experience trading both futures and options?

23. Would you prefer a 10% chance of making £10,000 or a 90% chance of making £1000. would it make any difference if the 90% chance was for £1,100, not just £1000?

24. How do you feel after a string of 5 losses?

25. When you lose is it usually the fault of someone else? Please explain.

26. Do you frequently take your broker's advice on the markets?

27. If so what are the results?

28. Do you examine your brokerage statements carefully?

29. Please set out a summary of your trading experiences with dates

C. Results

1. Do you make losses overall?

2. If so are you trading more than a single contract?

3. Do you see any logic in continuing to do so?

4. Do your losses arise from lots of small losses or a few big losses?

Note: **It is sometimes said that novice traders make a few big losses (because they fail to take small losses quickly), while more experienced traders make many small losses (because they put stops too tight). An adjunct to this is that very experienced derivative fund managers often lose in absolute terms because their clients take money away when they lose thus they make money on smaller sums than when they lose money.**

5. Do you think your problems stem from inexperience or from fear?

6. Or do you attribute this to other factors?

7. Do you take full responsibility for your trading actions and results?

8. If not, who is responsible?

9. Do your profits come from many small profits, or a few big profits? if you are not yet profitable which do you feel will apply to you?

10. Do you buy on good news?

11. If so, why?

12. Is it rare that the markets cause you any major problems?

13. Do you only ever lose what you plan in the markets?

14. When you lose more, are there good reasons? Please list.

15. If a great opportunity arises will you risk most of your money on it?

16. Explain why most traders are fugitives from the law of averages.

17. Do you love the thrill of trading, whether you win or lose?

18. Is trading your hobby?

19. If you lose do you want to get back at the market?

20. Do you usually act impulsively?

21. Do you hold your investments through thick and thin, do you have no problem holding in a bear market?

22. Do you talk about your trading results to anyone?

23. Do you keep a clear written record of all your trades and results?

24. Do you keep a journal listing all the reasons why you open and close trades?

25. If not, why not?

26. Are you a net loser over the last five years (or less if you have been trading for less than 5 years)?

D. Perception

1. Should a good system produce profits each month?

2. If the dartboard method works would you use it?

3. Do you regularly follow the advice of others?

4. Are you often confused?

5. Do you feel you have to be an insider to win?

6. Do you feel worthless unless you win?

7. Will you do a lot not to upset your broker?

8. Do you believe in random trading?

9. An orang-utan at San Diego zoo is calling the market with 86% accuracy. Do you follow the ape?

10. If you had to liken the market to an animal, real, imaginary or otherwise, what animal would it be?

11. What is your view of market systems?

12. Do you believe that once you find *your* system you will be successful?

13. Or do you believe that once you become a good trader that everything else will follow?

14. Have you mapped out the trading objectives you need to achieve? Not financial targets, but the lessons you need to learn. As an example, it may run: learn to cut losses, develop a methodology, learn to follow it, learn to run profits, become expert in this approach.

15. List those things you feel have meaning in the market.

16. How do you use these to make money?

E. Current situation

1. Could you live off your investments at this time?

2. How much time do you have for the market?

3. Do you ever miss trades because you are not paying sufficient attention?

4. How do you feel about that?

5. Do you get emotionally involved with the market?

6. If so, to what extent?

7. Is this useful?

8. What action do you propose to avoid this problem?

9. Are you often compelled to trade?

10. Do you often feel no need to trade?

11. How many contracts are you trading?

12. When you lose on a trade what percentage of your capital is lost?

13. Explain why you think this is the right level of risk for you?

14. Explain the statistical implications of this level of risk?

15. How many winning trades do you make on average, as a percentage of your trades in total?

16. Explain the statistical implications of this percentage allied to your level of risk.

17. Do you overspend?

18. What percentage of your capital is involved in trading?

F. Personal

1. Do you and your partner ever argue?

2. Do you enjoy meeting new people?

3. Are you a winner?

4. Are most of your friends winners also?

5. Do you ever lie?

6. Do you regularly list your goals, trading and otherwise?

7. Do you feel it is unlikely that you will attain any of your goals?

8. Do you have many close friends?

9. Is there anything that you are afraid to talk about?

10. Do you like everyone you know?

11. Do you love everyone you know?

12. When you do something do you dislike others to benefit?

13. Do you eat too much?

14. Do you smoke too much?

15. Do you drink alcohol to excess?

16. Do you take drugs to excess?

17. Do you engage in other self destructive behaviour?

18. Do you know why?

19. If you answered yes to any of questions 13 to 18 it would be useful if you gave more details. But do not feel obliged to do so.

20. Do you get on well with your work colleagues?

21. Do your work colleagues like you?

22. Do you regularly take holidays?

23. Have you ever felt better than you do now?

24. Do you more often see (a) other people's uses or (b) other people's viewpoints?

25. Do you feel uncomfortable going against the majority view?

26. If everyone in a room had removed their shoes would you do the same?

27. Are you afraid to face the reality of yourself?

28. Are you in touch with your own feelings?

29. Are you under pressure to succeed, either from yourself or others?

30. Are you relaxed when you trade?

31. Are you jealous of anyone?

32. In a confused situation would you turn to another for advice?

33. Why?

34. Is wealth important to you?

35. How would you define being wealthy?

36. How much time do you spend on newspapers?

37. What do they do for you?

38. Do you equate money to love?

39. If so, why?

40. Are you fit?

41. What exercise do you do?

42. Do you feel that it is important to be physically fit to trade markets?

43. If so, why?

44. What does money mean to you?

SALLY'S GURUS

John Bartlett: www.learntrading.co.uk

Sandy Jadeja: www.spreadbettingtowin.com

John Piper: www.john-piper.com

Greg Secker: www.knowledgetoaction.co.uk

Thanks also to David Graeme-Smith (www.shortswingtrading.com) who has always been extremely helpful and got left on the cutting-room floor through no fault of his own.

SALLY'S MINI-GLOSSARY

STOP LOSS - An order placed to limit losses on a bet.

GUARANTEED STOP LOSS – You place an order to ensure your bet is closed at the price you specify, even if the market gaps through the price. There is a small charge.

GAPS THROUGH - Occurs when the market trades through the level specified by you in an order, without actually trading at that given level.

ACKNOWLEDGEMENTS

Special thanks are due to Beverly Swerling Martin, who has never lost faith in my ability to write – even when I was harbouring doubts of my own.

Next on the Roll of Honour is Mel Croucher, my Big Brother and wonderful webmaster.

I am also indebted to Marianne Jones, for her helpful, incisive comments at every stage of the story. You're right, Marianne, I'd write faster if I drank less coffee.

Thanks, too to Francesca Drake. You know her better as Supermum.

My agent, Henry Morrison, has yet to fix me up with a date with Matt Damon, but we do have a novel to sell – and I suppose that has to take priority.

Tim Whiting is the best financial adviser a girl – or boy – could ever have. He's a million times better with money than I am, and it's thanks to Tim that I'm able to buy enough time to write.

At Finspreads, Gareth Robertson, Jo Benton, Katherine McGuinness and Kunjal Shah are always tremendously helpful in making sure I don't get locked up by the Financial Services Authority for saying the wrong thing.

And – of course – I am extremely grateful to all at Harriman House: Commissioning Editor Stephen Eckett, Managing Director Myles Hunt, and Helen McCusker and Tom Orchard in the PR Department who have promised to try and get me on Richard and Judy.

Camden Council isn't all bad. My local library, in Primrose Hill, is a wonderful asset to the community and I would like to thank the staff – particularly Myra, James, Colin and Costas - for their help and support with my writing.

Finally, Carol Clifford in Primrose Hill and Miriam Rankin in New York, who have both been fantastically supportive – and all my friends at groups.yahoo.com/group/awgrad.